Walking Without Footprints

To Jean Johnson and family

Connie Delaney

Walking Without Footprints
Going Native in America

Connie Delaney

Writers Advantage
New York   Lincoln   Shanghai

Walking Without Footprints
Going Native in America

All Rights Reserved © 2002 by Connie Delaney

No part of this book may be reproduced or transmitted in any form or by any means, graphic, electronic, or mechanical, including photocopying, recording, taping, or by any information storage retrieval system, without the permission in writing from the publisher.

Writers Advantage
an imprint of iUniverse, Inc.

For information address:
iUniverse
2021 Pine Lake Road, Suite 100
Lincoln, NE 68512
www.iuniverse.com

ISBN: 0-595-24660-5

Printed in the United States of America

To my memories of Ray Kelley, Wayne Shull, and all the old mountain men who taught them how to teach me.

And especially to the brave Wayne Talmadge, who looks after me now.

Contents

Chapter One	Cracking Buckets	1
Chapter Two	How to Find a Meadow	13
Chapter Three	How to Set Up a Tipi	22
Chapter Four	Tipi Living	32
Chapter Five	How a Cabin Finds You	43
Chapter Six	The Claim	52
Chapter Seven	How to Eat a Tree	63
Chapter Eight	Breathing in the Cold	72
Chapter Nine	How to Pray for a Meal	81
Chapter Ten	How to Howl at the Moon	91
Chapter Eleven	How to Move an Outhouse	99
Chapter Twelve	How to Find Financial Insecurity	109
Chapter Thirteen	Working the Claim	119
Chapter Fourteen	How to Flute a Moose	128
Chapter Fifteen	How Life Finds You	138
Chapter Sixteen	Keep on Walking	144
Chapter Seventeen	Flash Forward	154
Chapter Eighteen	Living Native in America	164
Chapter Nineteen	The Environmentalist and the Fox	168
Chapter Twenty	What I Learned from Cougar	178
Chapter Twenty-One	Walking without Footprints	188

Chapter One

Cracking Buckets

Life is never still. It runs like water in a frozen stream: solid on the surface, but running free underneath. When I try to look forward to what will happen, I can't see around the next bend. It's a mystery. Looking back I find little pools and eddies, stories with plot and resolution that seem to defy any order of occurrence. Meanwhile, with every breath, I am transfixed to the present moment, a wave rising up from the ocean of the universe, leaving droplets of myself behind, cresting towards the unknown.

The journey you are about to read is about me going in circles, finding myself the way a dog chases its tail. A spiraling dance that leads to the center. I write with the laughter of the dizzy.

Let's start with me high in a canyon, in the mountains of central Colorado. The elevation is almost 10,000 feet. It's late October and the first snows of winter have stuck permanently to the ground. Two cars are parked in a small depression off the dirt road. One is cold and layered with snow. The other, bare of ice with a still-warm engine. Maybe it's 1974 and, if that's true, I'm 20 years old. My hair is black, parted down the middle and plaited into long braids. I peer out of wire-rimmed glasses, the thin, metal arms curled firmly around my ears. These glasses are several years old, scratched and in need of a new prescription; the lenses are glass and heavy enough to leave a pink indentation on both sides of my nose. I'm wearing jeans, a shirt, a sweater, a coat and a stocking cap, all bought at the Goodwill store in Leadville.

It's cold. The air is crisp. We are near the continental divide, practically two miles high. This thin high-altitude air holds no heat and bites the lungs. It seems as if you can touch the cold in this kind of winter, see it perform its tricks. But it wasn't as cold as it was going to get. This was only the mild period of early winter. It seemed cold because we still had memories of summer. True cold, Joe told me, is when you dip a bucket into a running creek and it snaps into ice instantly.

I was no stranger to winter in the Rocky Mountains. I had grown up in the low lands, in the suburbs of Denver, which boasts itself to be a mile high. As a mountain girl now, I knew that a mile high was nothing. I'd lived one winter on the high plains of Buena Vista, Colorado, and one in Leadville, where the second step of the courthouse was two miles high. We were now just a few hundred feet shy of that. I knew cold from first-hand experience, but I'd only heard about freezing buckets from Joe, an obvious sign that I had spent my winters living indoors.

Bev and Joe were camping in this canyon, here in the snow. I was visiting for the evening from my warm home in town. Bev and I were best friends. Joe and I hardly tolerated each other. "Humph," was all he ever said to me, unless it was a mumbled suggestion of how little I really knew about the outdoors. We silently fought over other strange things, such as pants and dog food. But right now, freezing buckets were the silent competition between Joe's sullen mumbles and my determined stares. So I decided to discover freezing buckets for myself. Camp needed water anyway, and I wanted to be useful.

Bev handed me a bucket, dented and black with soot on the outside. She looked as if she had been shopping in the same fine establishment as me. She was padded with a second layer of clothes and a corduroy hat with earflaps. Her hair was also braided, the kind of brown that had once been blond. Her glasses were also wire-rimmed.

I turned and followed the snowy path out of camp toward the stream. Trees were drooping down, heavy with their load of snow. The soles of my boots left a set of knobby footprints behind me. I could hear a gurgle of bubbling water from under the crust of ice that was hiding the stream.

Where did Joe get water? Footprints up and down the bank gave me no clue. I worked my way downstream until I found a hole big enough for the bucket. That'll do. I stepped carefully onto the snow-covered rocks near the hole, the nubs on my boots gripped tentatively to the ice.

I felt tall and far away from my feet as I bent to push the bucket into the hole and under the ice. I tilted the bucket so water could run in, then lifted it out, three-quarters full at least. The water was revolving in the bucket, still moving from its downward journey with the stream. I half-expected to hear a loud snap as water froze into an instant ice cube. But it didn't.

The cold yet runny water sloshed from the side as I inched back across the rocks toward the trail. I leaned forward and sat the bucket down in front of me. Then, using it for support, I picked my way off the frozen rocks. The water was still swirling. As it slowed it thickened into an icy mush, forming a crust around the rim at the top. Not exactly an instant freeze.

The outside temperature was close to zero. It had been cold all month, so the water in the stream was below its 32-degree freezing point, but still far from the crack-into-ice point. That's the thing about water. It can stay liquid in the stream if it's moving. As long as gravity pulls it downward it keeps running. But stop it in a bucket (or splash it on a rock) and you find it was ice all the time.

Scientifically very interesting; existentially a point to prove my level of toughness.

I carried the bucket back to camp and balanced it against the fire to thaw, blackening the sides even more. I reached out my hands to warm them too. It was late afternoon, getting towards dusk.

Joe sneered at my mushy bucket, "Not even cold yet." He squatted by the fire making a show of pushing coals around, his head characteristically bent, scowling.

Joe didn't have secondhand clothes. His had to be at least third or fourth hand. Buying from a secondhand store was too extravagant for Joe. His probably came from a trashcan somewhere. I could see bony knees, covered with a layer of long underwear, sticking through a hole in his dirty pants.

"Barely fall still," he muttered and turned away. A limp strand of dark hair, which had escaped from the rubber band at the back of his neck, was plastered to his beard, frozen in place, like his attitude. It was obvious that my presence in his territory was not to his liking. He stood quickly and slunk off, out of sight.

We watched him go. Now we could talk. Bev was ecstatic I had found their camp. Not an easy task on my part, as I had found my way in by following short directions on a post card. I hadn't seen her for months. We quickly filled each other in on the details of our lives. I was working at a mine in Leadville; the second female ever to be hired at the Blackbird. Bev and Joe were going to winter out here on Homestake Creek.

She showed me the tipi someone had given them. It was a folded mass in the back of their car. The lump of blankets on the seat was their 10-month-old baby, Chance. He was a chance, all right. The bundle moved softly, like a sleeping baby should.

Bev had a look in her eye as she watched the baby, a look I'd never seen in her before. She was proud. She was protective. Her face was dirty from the campfire. Her long, ash-brown hair braided into thin strands with split ends sticking out. She had on layers of old used clothes, but she had a glow about her. She looked strong, normal. We turned away from the car and Bev led me over to the pile of poles that Joe was peeling for their winter home.

The poles didn't look very peeled to me. They were lumpy and crusty. "And he only got 12 of them," worried Bev. "I don't know if that will hold the tipi up through the snow. Joe says it's a small tipi and doesn't need the full 18."

I had read about tipis also, and was wondering how they were going to sit out a winter in a 12-footer. This was considered the tiniest size by real Indians (according to my white-man reading sources), used only on fast moving hunting trips. But what did I know? Joe had sufficiently humbled me with the water bucket. I had never camped when the buckets froze instantly, so I couldn't pretend to know anything.

The baby woke up.

Bev started cooking up some beans and taking care of him. I helped as best as I could, but really did nothing more than stoke the fire and push the coals around. The sun was slanting down towards evening. We ate our beans and talked about all the things we wanted to do. We had the best plans to live our lives well. Beans and a fire were the most we wanted. We would live without leaving the slightest trace of harm on our already polluted planet. We would *become* the wilderness itself, living the life a natural human was meant to live. Chance went back to sleep, tucked in a blanket against Bev's chest. The fire warmed us from the front. Our dreams warmed us inside.

Bev and Joe were going to sleep in the car again that night; they'd been there for a week. Tomorrow they would pitch the tipi, but not on this side of the creek. At first they thought they would stay here, but there was a place more secluded over on the other side, away from the road.

I couldn't stay. The best thing for me was to head back to my little house in Leadville, about an hour's drive away. I was in a borrowed car. I had to get it back.

It was starting to get dark. Bev and I walked out to the road, where we could see Homestake Creek. She pointed the direction to the new camp to make sure I could find it. Go down a bit, around the bend; there's a log over the creek. Past that is a campground. Go into the campground, down to the creek, and I'll find rocks to get across. Climb the bank on the other side to a small meadow. Easy. I'd found Bev before. I could do it again.

The winter dusk settled around us as we stoked the fire. Bev squinted into the darkness beyond the fire, looking for Joe. Where had he gone?

She rocked the baby and chattered, complaining softly about the way Joe acted, glancing often down the trail where his hunched form had disappeared into the snow.

He came back as the first stars were showing through the trees. Still barely speaking, head down. He'd *just* been on a walk.

Time for me to go. I made my quick goodbyes and drove back to town where a warm house awaited me, but it wasn't what I wanted. I longed to live in the woods, wild, like Bev and Joe. In my imagination they were as warm and cozy as I was. Soon, I'd do it too.

Freedom. That's what it was about. Bev and Joe (and me too) were trying to find the free, natural way to live. You may think we were going to extremes, and you'd be right. But extremism can be a good way to find the truth about something. As Thoreau said one time, describing why he went to live at Walden Pond, we wanted to live away from the "expectations of society." Mostly we wanted to live away.

I had been longing for freedom for a long time. I grew up in city suburbs in the sixties. That world was made of identical square houses with patches of lawn. It was shockingly obvious to me that people weren't natural. More than that, we didn't seem to have a clue how to *be* natural. What was the human animal about? What were we doing? We (actually, "They") had become a mass machine, intent on blowing up the world with nuclear bombs. Or polluting it to death. I wanted out.

Bev agreed with me; Joe too. He was the real expert. There was only one problem with Joe: in the wild search for freedom he had discounted the fact that he was also Homo sapiens—a white, formerly middle-class, American one at that. Just a small oversight that led to eventual downfall. But that is not part of the beginning of the story.

I wanted to be free like a bird, or a deer. I thought that meant living like a bird or a deer. It may be a bit silly if you look at it logically. But don't be too hard on us, it's not like we had a ton of role models to choose from. It is rare to find a free human being. Only the Zen masters can tell us about it.

The Urge

There is a Zen story called the "Ten Bulls." Actually, it is a series of ten paintings—a cartoon from ancient Japan. It's an illustration of my life.

In the first painting we meet our hero. He is standing by his bullpen with a look of dismay. His bull is gone! The unlatched gate swings open. He gazes at the empty pen in shock and fear. How could his bull be gone? Who left the gate open?

This painting shows how we awaken to the spiritual path, the wandering path. The bull represents spirituality, Tao, soul, or whatever you want to call it. Often we are so busy with the details of our lives that we forget to tend the bull. We leave the gate open and it escapes. Sometimes, as happens with our hero, a great deal of time passes before anyone notices it has escaped. It's long gone, and there is no telling which direction it went.

Sometimes a person can feel that something has been missing in their life for a long time. They never think to look in the bullpen. In fact, they may even forget there ever was a bullpen. Then something happens and they discover the bull is lost; they feel the center of their being is lost. This is what happens to the hero of our story. There is only one thing to do.

Picture number two shows the man off in search of his bull. He carries a walking stick and a bag. He looks pretty spiffy—off on an adventure.

In the next pictures our hero searches high and low for his lost bull. In each consecutive frame he looks a little more ragged. He catches sight of hoof prints. Then he sees the tail, and, at last, the whole bull.

With a great lunge, our hero catches the beast and wrestles it into submission. In the eighth and ninth frame he leads his prize back home and locks it securely in the pen, celebrating.

We think we are modern now, but the journey is the same. When we realize our bull is lost, a great desire arises to find it. Go on a search and there are traces to be found. Follow those traces and the creature itself will appear. If you have any courage at all, you'll make a grab for the beast. Once you've caught the bull, it gladly follows you home.

You'd think this would be the end of the story. The elusive bull is caught and the whole affair ought to be finished. But our ancient Eastern friends were wiser than that. After all, they had caught their bulls, in that time long ago. They knew what would happen after.

It's something different than you'd expect. The tenth bull of Zen is hard to believe. In fact, many Zen traditions refuse to acknowledge it as part of the series. They toss it out and pretend there are only nine bulls. The last concept didn't fit the aspirations of the "holier-than-thou" priesthood.

The last painting shows our hero again. The bull is safely in the pen, happily munching on hay. Our hero has grabbed a bottle of wine and is off to celebrate in the marketplace. He has a happy, drunken smile on his face. He rejoins the bustle of humanity, an ordinary man—celebrating with the best wine! We wouldn't be able to tell the difference between this guy and the folks at the AA meeting. Only difference is that *his* bull is home in the pen.

You may think this is a bunch of bull, but the meaning is pretty clear. If your spirit is lost, you need to find it. It's a solitary journey. Thoreau said it well, "I have some private business to transact, and I want to do it deliberately." Go ahead and look. Look with your eyes open. Make a good, hard search. Put one hundred percent of yourself into it so that you aren't doing it forever. When you catch that sucker, pen him up and get on with life. Cheers!

It amazes me that some painter, thousands of years ago in the East, drew a cartoon of my life. Did he know I would wake up in my last year of high school and find my bull was gone? Did he know I'd be searching for it by a frozen mountain stream? Do you think he knew that the little seeds of my discontent were sown all through my young life? I wonder.

I've always had a romantic vision of the wilderness. My mother loved to take her whole brood camping, so I was fortunate to have had an experience of it. My first real passion struck as a small child reading the book,

My Side of the Mountain. The boy in this book jumps on a bus, rides out of New York City and lives in a hollow tree for a year. He has a falcon for a friend and gets buried in snow.

I could do that.

You can slip back further through time to find how I lost my bull. Maybe it never had a chance from the beginning. Many events shaped me in those younger years. We all think we are individuals, but in many ways we aren't. We are a part of our time, molded by the winds of change and whims of society.

My parents were born to a world of hope and then challenged by the depression. Early days of poverty formed an electric connection with the brain cells that govern action. "Work cures everything," was the motto. Then, boom. World War II.

This war focused the genius and resources of humanity into astounding technological advances. Atoms sliced themselves in the air in a grand finale—a tremendous flash annihilating two Japanese cities, spewing nuclear waste into the air in giant mushroom clouds. It happened before I was born, but it has colored every minute of my days.

That war shifted humanity into high gear. We could lift more, dig more, chop more, build more, and do more than ever before. Western nations wallowed in their wealth. Everything boomed, especially babies. I was born into the largest generation in history. More babies and more wealth than ever before. The dream had come true.

But someone wasn't watching. As Jesus says, "If the blind lead the bind, they both fall into the pit." The Depression Generation did a great job, but they forgot one little detail—if everything on the planet was used up for this baby boomer generation, there would be nothing left for their children. (It must be this same human blindness which led my generation to try to save the world for future generations while forgetting to take care of our actual children. Oops.)

By the mid-sixties, problems were starting to become obvious. Birds weren't singing in the trees. Cancer and heart disease had become top killers. World population reached four billion, and mathematicians published figures of how fast it would keep growing (30 years later reality has more than met with speculation). A terrifying war was brewing in the jungles of the East. We had built enough bombs to blow up the whole planet seven times over. It was no secret.

These things sent my bull-dashing for cover. I remember hiding under my desk in third grade nuclear-raid drills. The siren would go off every Friday so we could practice. We left our books on top of our desks and got under them until the "all-clear" sounded. It was a pretty big thing for a third grader to deal with. I always thought, if the Russians decided to bomb us they would surely do it on Friday, 2:45 p.m., because then we would be fooled into thinking the air raid sirens were only for a practice. What if they were really bombing this time? What else do you think about when you are nine and waiting for nuclear bombs to hit? Not much.

Later, I asked my teacher why third grade hid under their desks and first and second grade ran for the basement. She told me there wasn't enough room in the basement for everyone.

"Well," I had to ask, "is hiding under the desk going to do any good?"

"No, it won't," she replied.

"Will hiding in the basement do any good?"

"Maybe."

I've got to hand it to my teacher for her honesty. There wasn't enough room for me in the basement. It was a piece of information that never found a comfortable place to settle in the brain. Sometimes I still think there isn't enough room for me.

As terrible as that may seem, a big shake-up isn't necessarily a bad thing for the human brain. Several pieces of information that don't fit into a comfortable pattern can spark a transcendence that gets the bull in a roving mood. The fact that you (and your whole planet) could get bombed to pieces any minute brings a certain awareness. Stop! you want to shout.

There is a Zen meditation where the disciple gets yelled at a couple of times a day—STOP! This "stop" catches him unaware and brings a moment of realization. In the time called the "Bay of Pigs" humanity had a big "stop" meditation. The day our president, John Kennedy, was killed we had another stop. It did something to everyone. I was a small child—it did something to me.

I remember, later: sitting in Catholic school in my uniform. We'd just been taught about China. Some of the pictures in our books showed Chinese children playing. We're told there are a billion Chinese, and math helps us learn how many a billion really is. Then it's religion class, and we are told that little children who aren't baptized Catholic will have to go to limbo when they die. They are not bad enough to go directly to hell, but limbo is a pretty bad place. I look at the pictures of the Chinese children in my book and know that this piece of information just can't be true: all those cute little children can't go to heaven just because they are Chinese children? I see a lie and I calmly know it—I had the brains to keep my mouth shut.

Another point—I was a teenager, awash in the belief that I knew everything: walking up a hill one day, the rush of blood from my beating heart makes me dizzy and gives things a different look. I suddenly realize how my own perception colors the world. Maybe there were things I didn't know. Change the perception and you change the color. It was just a brief moment, but a great illumination.

That hill is a photograph forever in my mind, as are the Chinese children in my sociology books. Simple moments that meant something to me. I think revelations happen in everyone's life just like that. It's normal, like breathing. Sometimes it is so obvious we discount it. We are more mystical than we know.

One time I was in my bedroom. I had a forbidden deck of Tarot cards and a book on Eastern mysticism. I threw the cards about my future and got the "Fool" card. Then I read the book and learned the idea of enlightenment for the first time. The bull was dancing that day. With that wonderful folly of youth I decided right there: I was going to be enlightened in my lifetime.

I could do that.

Transcendence sounded like a simple idea at the time. It was in a book, so it's gotta be true. Right? It's no wonder I got the Fool card.

One other decisive day. It was Sunday, after church. My dad loaded all six of us kids in the back of the station wagon, Mom in front, and we went for a drive up Clear Creek Canyon into the mountains. We drove a little while, then got out of the car for a hike down a trail. We hiked along, a happy Catholic family: kids, mom, and dad. Suddenly we came into an open meadow that was full of naked hippies running around and splashing in the stream. My dad turned with the swiftness of total father-like determination, herding his brood together, quickly out of the meadow. But I was the second oldest, and taller. I stretched my head and eyes to see: a meadow of naked hippies. They were having fun. I had never seen such fun being had before, but knew, instinctively, that what they were doing was majorly fun. My dad tried with the utmost of his strength to protect his brood from such a sight, but it was too late. I'd seen. I decided, then and there, *that's what I want to be when I grow up.* Up until that point I had wanted to be an astrophysicist.

I had no doubts that I could be whatever I wanted to be. Astrophysicist? Naked hippie? I could live in a tree in the winter and I could be enlightened. Life goals were being set.

So, who would be surprised that, at the age of 18, I grew out my hair, shouldered a backpack, and started hiking to the mountains, a white, middle class, American Indian-wannabe Buddha, heading for the wild lands. Looking for icy buckets and transcendence.

Chapter Two

How to Find a Meadow

I first met Bev in Denver in 1971. We were the younger hippies—too young for civil rights marches and Woodstock. I was still in high school. We'd seen the drug trip and were tired of shaking-zombie friends. She was Crazy Bev to me, and besides that she was a nurse. She had a small trust fund and a Kharmen Ghia. I assumed she acted pretty normally when she was being a nurse, but off work she was just crazy. That girl would do anything—and hence the name: "Crazy Bev."

As young girls we had the gall to believe we could be free people. (Go tell?...) It was my dream to go live out in the woods—out in the wild. I talked it over with Bev, night after night. Then one day I heard Bev had left town and was living in a small cabin up in the mountains. She had taken off before me!

Bev had met a guy named Joe and they were living off the land. Actually, they were living off Bev's trust fund, but why let reality cloud my story now? We didn't let it affect us then.

Joe was the scruffiest sort of hippie the era produced. He was short and skinny. His hair was long, straggly, and uncombed. His philosophy was, "less is better." From there it was easy enough to believe that less than less was even better. They drove the Kharmen Ghia around and collected aluminum cans for a living. Today they'd be called homeless, or street people. Back then it was a lifestyle choice. They thought they'd hit on a good deal.

It was the booming seventies for us young folk. Maybe the stock market guys were all stressed and nervous, but all we saw was the overabundant leavings of corporate America. It was our job, and our responsibility, to use this stuff up. We lived in a world that was so rich, a person could live off the garbage.

Did you know that trashcans are full of good stuff? Every day grocery stores throw out perfectly good food. Did you know that you can go around back and get what you want out of the dumpsters? Joe did. Did you know that the best and cheapest food to eat is dog food? You can buy it in big bags, it has all the nutrition you need, and you don't have to cook it!

I can still see Joe smiling as he offered me a taste from his bowl. Who needed a job? We saw the world as containing too much—so much that we could simply live off the leavings of the rich.

My sage advice to the young: Don't worry. There is still plenty of garbage!

Garbage

Dirt is a wonderful thing. When you live out in the woods, it is an integral part of life. In some ways, dirt is dangerous. It can be full of germs and ruins everything it touches. In another way, dirt is very healing. When you are really dirty you feel alive! Dirt means something's happened. You sweated, you rolled. You climbed and fell. Children dive into dirt given the chance. Adults covered with dirt feel like children.

You'd think that good old-fashioned dirt is something that can't be corrupted. You roll in the dirt, and then you wash it off. It's an experience. But even something as innocent as dirt can become oppression if forced on someone.

I remember visiting Bev once when Joe decided it was better to never wash clothes. It was the first spring they were together, before the baby, before any cold winters. They were living in a campground near Kanosha pass. I was still in Denver, just out of high school. Bev had mailed me a postcard with a little map to their camp, and that was all I needed to head up to the mountains. It was a beautiful May day. I talked a friend into giving me a ride. My friend drove me up and dropped me off at the mouth of the road. It was only a half-mile hike into the campsite.

Bev told me that they had gone to the Laundromat a couple weeks ago, and Joe noticed the lint left in the dryers when the clothes were finished. Concluding that this lint was little bits and pieces of his clothes that the dryer was taking away, he decided that clothes would last longer if never washed. Joe wasn't about to get ripped off.

This philosophy immediately became the religion for his family. No one was allowed to wash clothes. He scowled at my cleanliness. I was wasting perfectly good clothes by washing them. Not like Joe. His pants were thick, strong, and pure, not having been corrupted by laundering for a very long time. I bet he's got the same pair on to this day.

Bev's clothes had an acceptable amount of crust on them, though she confessed to me that she rinsed them in the nearby creek if ever Joe happened to be gone for the day. Since she was also not allowed to wear underpants (not necessary according to Joe), she was having a problem with dripping.

As usual, Joe couldn't stand me. As soon as I arrived in camp, he found some excuse to take off—and Bev and I scrubbed up some pants in the cold water from the creek. We hung them on a tree branch in the sun to dry. I guess we were rebelling against the rebel.

Joe had an interesting idea about the pants. I still wonder about it every time I clean the lint from a dryer. It was worth an experiment to find out how long a pair of jeans would last if never washed. Too bad he felt the need to force it on Bev.

How to Find a Cabin

The winter that Bev and Joe met each other they lived in a cabin with a bunch of other "hippies." They found this cabin by hanging out in the woods until they met someone who knew someone who was willing to have a caretaker in their summer vacation cabin.

This haphazard method is the best way I've discovered to find a great place to live. I've used it many times since then. People who are living in a place are the ones who know about it. Get to know them and you'll find a home. Always ask about sun and flood and winds.

The mountains and woods of the United States are full of summer cabins and old homesteads that are empty most of the time. These places are not lived in full time, especially in the winter, because people cannot support themselves out in the woods. Problem is, you probably can't support yourself out in the woods either—but we'll get into that later.

Houses that are not lived in get full of rats and dirt; they fall apart, and the yards are a mess. Caretakers can help keep up a place. If you want to move out in the woods for awhile it is easy to find a free place in which to live.

There are also good reasons for people not to have a caretaker for their cabin out in the woods. When I visited Bev and Joe's cabin after the first winter, they had trashed the place. It was a dark and dingy cabin anyway. Now, it looked like a battle zone. Bev, Joe, and their cabin-mates had left the place full of garbage, inside and out.

It had been quite a winter, I guess. Everyone had left in personal moments of crisis, chased from the mountain retreat by reality. Most of the problems were caused by snow up to the windows and no money (aluminum cans are hard to find in winter.)

My friend Bev was no exception. Her personal crises had spun her back to Denver, to get a job again as a nurse. Bev stayed with me until the snow first began to let up in the spring, and we drove the Kharmen Ghia back to the scene of destruction. Joe was off somewhere.

I was shocked. My parents owned a vacation cabin in Wyoming. It was a source of pride for us. We had a law so firm that it could never be broken—the cabin must be immaculate before leaving. The last day of any vacation was a clean-up ritual that ended with sweeping out the door so not the slightest footprint of dirt was left inside. If you had to go back in for something—you swept yourself out again. No footprints left in that cabin.

Bev's cabin hadn't been swept for six months. Moldy clothes lay in piles in the corners. We made a half-hearted attempt to clean up. There was no water, so we drove to a local store with a bunch of buckets and filled up. It wasn't enough to make a difference in the look of the place but we washed the dishes and arranged piles of junk that were lying around. In one of the piles of clothes I found a long black flute case. I opened it up and there was a nice Artley flute. Bev said it probably belonged to a girl from California. Chances were certain that she would never be coming back. I had learned to play flute in grade school. It seemed only logical that the flute should become mine.

When we ran out of water, we gave up. We cooked a pot of rice and ate it plain (that's all there was, no wonder everyone left.)

There you have it. We were the generation angry about how our parents were trashing the whole planet, and yet couldn't keep one small place clean.

The next morning Joe showed up to get Bev. It was my first time to meet him, and neither of us was impressed with the other. He didn't say much to me, and I returned the favor.

Joe had accumulated quite a stash of aluminum cans, which he kept in five large garbage sacks behind the cabin. He showed them off with pride, the way a cat shows off its captured mouse. He had been waiting for Bev to come back with the car so he could smash them. Proudly, he demonstrated his innovative technique for compacting aluminum cans. He threw them all over a pull-off down by the highway and drove the car back and forth over them. Bev and I gathered the cans up into sacks and crammed them into the trunk and back seat of the Ghia.

Cleaning Vision

Cleaning has not been a priority for human beings—at least as far as recognition and income is concerned. I have one hope for mankind. I'd like to see us all stand up tall and declare that cleaning is the most honorable profession. Let's clean the nuclear waste and the toilets too. Let's weed empty lots in the cities and plant flowers. If we want our world to be paradise, somebody has to make it so. Cleaning is an art form. We should applaud and honor the cleaners. We can make our neighborhoods and houses sparkle like a clear mountain stream. We can make our cleaners happy people instead of the backwash of society, as they are today.

Benedictine monks have a rule—everyone helps in the kitchen: the highest visiting dignitary and the lowest novice, washing dishes together, cutting vegetables. It's a meditation. This is a rule that could transform our economically stratified society. What if you went to a fancy dinner, paid a hundred dollars for the meal, and then went back into the kitchen and helped the cook stir the soup for a little while. You would get to chat with the people who had made your food. It could even be fun.

There is a lesson to be learned from that first cabin, though I only stayed one day. It takes a lot of energy and resources to keep a place clean. It takes even more to clean up something that has been trashed. And, most of all: It is a very simple thing to turn away from a mess if you didn't make it.

UP THE MOUNTAIN

This brings us back to the beginning of winter in 1974 and the crackling snow of Homestake creek. I had gone back to my little rented house in Leadville, but I wanted to go be with Bev, again, in her tipi. Several weeks after my first visit I decided to hike in and look for their camp. This time I was prepared to stay a few nights. I had a pack, a sleeping bag, and food.

The snow was deeper now. I wanted to see the tipi, now that it was up. I got a ride to the start of the Homestake Creek road and hiked in the last four miles with my pack. I found my way to their old camping spot, and then it was just as Bev had described. Up around the next bend a side road headed down into a Forest Service campground. I followed that down to the creek and found a nice wide spot with plenty of rocks for crossing. I picked my way across—slipping and wetting my boot on the ice covered rocks—climbed the bank, and found the tipi.

Bev was glad to see me. Joe slunk off.

Things were not going so well in paradise. This camping site was more secluded than the first spot, yes. But it was also hidden in the trees, cold and gray, with no sun. After they pitched the tipi here, they realized their mistake. Then Joe found a better meadow down stream. Bev described it with a wistful look in her eye—a big meadow where the morning sun would find the camp. The creek was narrow down there, with high banks, and there was a perfect log across the creek for access, much better than crossing slippery rocks. They thought of moving, but one week of snow had frozen the bottom of the tipi firmly to the ground. Moving the tipi was a lot of effort for Joe to undertake. Joe was not big into effort.

Apparently, I had interrupted a long-running argument. The buckets were freezing pretty quick now, but there was no joy in the camp. The usually vivacious Bev was thin-lipped and quiet. We crawled in through the doorflap of the tipi where it was smoky and crowded. To make a space for my pack and sleeping bag, Bev had to cram their bed over to the side. I was taking up a lot of space.

A 12-foot tipi isn't too comfortable. We didn't want to stay inside any longer than necessary. We crawled back outside and set about the chores, gathering willow wood for the fire and cooking dinner.

While we ate, the sun sank below the treetops to the west. The temperature dropped. It was barely five o'clock, but the day was done. We crawled into the little tipi. The smoke wasn't rising very well inside, even though Joe had dug a trench and buried a piped-air vent system made out of old cans. I coughed and rubbed my eyes and finally lay down with my nose near the ground to escape the smoke. Around the fire I listened to Bev and Joe argue silently, without words.

I slept, crowded with the unhappy couple in the tipi that night. Somehow it was the last straw. The next morning Bev announced that she was out of there. She was heading back to civilization with me.

All hell broke loose. Joe wanted to keep the baby so he could raise him as a true free spirit in the wilderness. Chance (remember the baby?) was in his backpack carrier. Bev and Joe each grabbed one end of the hapless infant's carrier and started pulling and screaming—trying to gain control. They were out in the woods trying to live like the free deer and birds, but had brought all the violence and control of humanity along with them.

Joe was a small man. I jumped in on Bev's side and we won custody. Joe backed off. Bev immediately slung the backpack with the baby onto her back and cinched the belt on her waist to prove ownership. Chance was quiet—he didn't make a sound. Bev picked up a bag containing the only possessions she was bringing from this life and clutched it in her arms. I slung my backpack on my shoulders and grabbed an armful of blankets. We headed off through the snow.

Joe gave in and followed along. The few times I chose to look I could see him behind us, carrying a load he had thrown together. We were shy and cautious after the outburst, walking in silence to the highway where the Kharmen Ghia was parked.

Bev and Joe agreed on only one thing. To give *me* the tipi. They were both heading somewhere else. Bev and I drove off in the car with the baby. Joe stuck out his thumb, heading the other direction.

Bev dropped me at my little house in Leadville. I never saw either one of them again. I tried, once or twice, to find Bev, asking mutual acquaintances. Finally one friend told me she *did* know where Bev was, but that she was hiding from Joe. For protection, this friend had sworn never to reveal Bev's location to anyone—especially someone that knew Joe. So Bev, if you ever read this, Hi. My best to you. You live favorably in my thoughts, and thanks for the tipi.

Chapter Three

How to Set Up a Tipi

Early the next spring I caught a ride to the Homestake Creek Road and backpacked in to find my tipi. With me, this time, were the friends I had acquired through the winter: two young dogs, Levi and Sheela, and Stubby the cat.

Stubby was a calico cat whose tail had been pulled off at birth. Her mother's anxious owner had tried to help the birth process by pulling on the first available piece of kitten. Sitting, stunned, with the kitten tail in his hand, and the kitty yet to show, he became an immediate proponent of natural childbirth and let the rest of the kitties come out by themselves. Meanwhile, Stubby gained certain notoriety and only a stub of a tail with which to express her innermost thoughts.

Levi was a cagey puppy, part Border collie and part coyote. Sometimes a bit too clever for her own good, she took up lead position. Sheela was the wisest and most sober of us all. Part husky and part German shepherd, she was black from tip to toe. Sheela was our guard and watched carefully that all members of the party stayed together and behaved themselves. Stubby did what she wished, sometimes joining the procession, sometimes hiding in the bushes. Occasionally, I would have to go back, pick her up and carry her for a ways. I was running away from people but far from alone. Companionship was all over my ankles as I hiked.

Winter still gripped to the land as dirty mounds of spring snow clung in shady spots under trees and near the mountain cliffs. I clomped along in my trusty new boots: Redwing high-tops, Vibram soles. I had really splurged on this footgear. Something I rarely did was to spend money on something new, but I had actually bought these shoes in a store. It was my extravagance. There is nothing like a new pair of boots on your feet to gain a feeling of security.

An old army type backpack was hitched over my shoulders. A cotton sleeping bag swung from the bottom. I had a good supply of rice, beans, oats, and cheese. I was free and happy, with $500 stuffed in my pocket.

I had worked through the winter at a mine in Leadville—my first job at real-man wages, which was something like $3.00 an hour at the time. That, in itself, was an eye-opening experience. When you work for man wages (as opposed to girl wages or minimum wage) the money stacks up fast. Three months at that job and I had enough to live for a year. Five hundred bucks was a big wad.

The spring sun shone happily on my shoulders for the four-mile hike. Everything was sparkling. The trees, water, and rocks looked pleased. Purple Pasque flowers grew on the downward side of patches of snow. There was no trace of the darkness that had engulfed my trip to see Bev and Joe last winter. The road headed through trees, then broke into a long open meadow. I strode along the straight of the road, then around the bend into the beginnings of the forest.

The log over the creek was easy to find. I could see it from the road. It straddled the water where the banks were close together and steep. The skinny, top end was on my side. The broken, uprooted base on the far side. Homestake Creek rushed deep and quick, a long way down.

I sat down to rest, drink some water, and survey the scene. The log seemed pretty skinny—plenty strong enough to hold my weight, but not wide enough for a safe foothold. The banks on each side were steep. My pride, and old, time-past voices of my brothers dared me on, wanted me to walk, standing up, across the log. My brain told me that I should be balanced enough to do it. Things I had read about yoga and spiritual beings insisted that being well-balanced meant being evolved.

I was alone. Falling here would not be good. Never mind.

I flipped my shoulders, resetting my heavy pack on my back, and stepped out on the log. My Vibram soles gripped tentatively to the moist wood. Looking down I could see the white water swirling over sharp rocks below.

Suddenly I'm floating upstream as the water churns past. Whoa. I step back.

What was more important? Walking deftly and gracefully across this log, showing off to the water and trees that I was a truly fearless and well-balanced person who could walk a log—or—definitely, one hundred percent, certainly, making it across safely?

That's not a real question.

I knelt down, gripped the log with my hands and crawled, inch by inch, across. On the other side I stood up. Good enough. Two dogs and a cat danced across without a second thought. Well gee. They didn't have packs.

I climbed up through the trees, and there, just as Joe had said, was the meadow with the sunshine that was to be my home. I wouldn't even think about spending the night in the dingy spot that had sent Bev and Joe running for town. I was going to put the tipi in this best meadow first thing.

I surveyed my territory and decided the tipi needed the early morning sun, I chose a flat, grassy spot to the far west end of the meadow and set down my pack. A quick walk through the woods to the south brought me to Bev and Joe's small clearing. The tipi had fallen from the poles and crusted to the ground with melted and frozen snow.

I wanted my home and I wanted it now. I took down the poles and dragged them, two at a time, to my new spot to begin raising them into position.

Raising Poles

A tipi is an amazing feat of engineering. It is based on a tripod, which creates the strongest foundation of any structure. Push, or pull down on a tripod and it only gets stronger. You can't tip it over from any side. It makes a good house if you can overcome a few difficulties. The poles shouldn't cross each other at the top of the cone because the smoke from the center fire, which wants to rise straight up, would get caught there. Also, rain, snow, and hail fall straight down, and you certainly don't want that coming into the house. If the hole was on the top it couldn't be plugged. A perfect cone would result in a lot of wet, smoky Indians. Fortunately, Indian engineers solved this problem many years ago. A well-set tipi is a tilted cone with the fire towards the front. Smoke rises through the short exposed edge, and rain rolls off the long back. Flaps at the top help channel wind currents to help the smoke rise, and can be closed in a heavy rain.

For me, a beginning wannabe Indian, the pole raising created a major problem. My only teacher in setting my tipi was a blue, hardbound copy of the tipi bible—"The Indian Tipi" by Reginald and Galdys Laubin. I was also in a hurry—it had taken most of the day to get into Homestake Creek and I wanted a home to sleep in that night.

I read the instructions in my book, and tackled the poles. The first part was easy: I lay three poles on the ground and tied them near the top. Two poles were bundled together and the third stretched across the campsite. The idea was to lift this assembly, pivoting up on two bases—and then pull the third pole into its place, creating the tripod. Remember, the join is about 12 feet high—the poles are over 14 feet. According to the book, I was supposed to have a helper pulling on the tie rope as I raised the poles. My friends, the dogs and cat, gave me blank looks.

There had to be a way to do it solo. I grabbed the poles where they were tied, lifted, and walked along the double set, pushing them higher and higher as I went. There came a point where the poles up in the air were heavier than the bases on the ground. The whole thing whizzed over my head and bit the dust.

Wiser, I started again. When I felt gravity begin to win, I gave a mighty heave and won the battle. The poles reached to the sky, standing vertical—only problem was that I was holding them. So far I'd only made a duo-pod. Two poles were in my hands, tied at the top to the third pole stretched across the camp. How do I pull the two poles apart, stretching them into the tripod and keep what I already had up—still up?

The two poles in my hands were equally heavy on the ground. I tried pushing and throwing one of them, only to end up dodging the butt end as it crashed to earth. The afternoon shadows were getting long. I was getting mad.

It was one of those moments in life where only a full vocabulary of swear words, combined with rabid innovation, would work. Anger and a touch of fear surged in my blood. I pushed one of the double poles up through the top knot, shortening it so it would swing easier once raised, grabbed the assembly and heaved it into air. Calling upon every disgusting part of the human anatomy, and deities to match, I swung the short pole through the air. Blood rushed to find enough capillaries in my lungs to get oxygen. I leapt with the pole in that split second it was airborne, swung, and ran with it into place. Hah! Tripod achieved!

I sat down, winded.

The strongest architectural base can be pretty tough to create. But there it was. I could push it. I could pull it. Winds could blow fierce and this thing would not fall down. Great. I pulled on the center rope to tighten the topknot and adjusted the base aimlessly. I couldn't tell if the thing was tilted right. I didn't care. I piled the rest of the poles in the top crotch, according to my tipi instructions. It was a simple matter of one, two, three, following the diagram around.

Now for the cover. I hiked back to Bev and Joe's old camp and surveyed the mess. My new home was still frozen in a snowy heap.

I pulled gently on the tipi cover shaking off the grainy spring snow. It came up pretty well except for one edge that was frozen in hard ice. I got a big stick (being fully primitive, of course, and having no axe) and started beating the ice, holding the material to the ground. Slowly, I managed to release winter's hold on my dwelling, although I severely ripped the bottom edges in a few places. I was going to be a pretty ragged-looking Indian.

I dragged the wet, unruly canvas through the woods to my clearing. And spread it out in the meadow to survey the damage.

A tipi cover is half a circle with smoke flaps sewn on the middle of the flat edge. Our handy Indian engineers of times past cut their tipi "patterns" with a giant handmade compass. They pounded a stake in the middle of a meadow, tied a long rope to it, laid their stitched-together skins up against the stake, and walked a half circle with the string, drawing the edge of their circular home as they went. Handy and practical.

According to my tipi bible, the lazy-old-men Indians had nothing to do with their homes, except live in them and paint the pictures on the outside. My tipi had no pictures. Of course, then again, I had no lazy old man around. The previous owner had been such a lazy old man he didn't even paint. It was a bare bones operation. Indian slums. No extra frills.

Attached to the top center of the cover was a small rope. I took my last pole, which is called the lifting pole, laid it out on the cover to measure, and tied it in place. Then I folded both sides of the tent inwards towards the poles, as in my instructions, and commenced to lift the thing into the air. It was heavy. Fortunately I was situated right with the tipi, and it fell into place in the top crotch.

According to my instructions, I was now supposed to walk the cover around both sides of the pole structure in an elegant show of female grace. Guess I hadn't done the folding right. The fabric twisted in wrong directions. I had to shake and twist the cover around the tripod. I ran from one side to the other, trying to get it right. I couldn't get the front to meet in the middle. Pushing the poles up to make the base of the tripod skinnier helped a bit. I strong-armed the edges together but could only get half the little sticks to fit through the center buttonholes at the middle seam. The sun slipped down through the treetops to the west.

I was a failure. The cover fit all wrong. There was a big gap at the bottom. One side was way up in the sky and the other side was dragging on the ground. The ragged, torn edge flapped in the breeze. Good thing there wasn't a whole tribe around to watch. I would have been the laughing stock of Homestake Creek.

I pushed the poles around to adjust the cover good enough for the night. A little ventilation wasn't going to hurt me. I was exhausted.

I somewhat inadequately tied the liner in place, set my bed in its proper spot and scraped out a little spot for a fire. I didn't build a fire inside though; remembering how smoky the tipi could get. I set a fire outside and cooked my small dinner of lentils and rice. Then I got out my flute and played quietly as the light slipped away and stars appeared in the mountain night. My belly was full with rice. I fed the flames of the fire with little sticks.

This was the total embodiment of my dream: food, clothing, and shelter. I had all the things necessary for survival. A perfect moment.

The stars shone bright on me that night, and I shone back. In my way, I was trying to be an example for all of humanity. (A big clue to the fact that I really hadn't had time yet to think it all out. One person, alone in a meadow, is not an example for a whole society. I learned later that minimal is not always best. But it's good to begin with a minimum and build.)

As I look at it now, I see that the basic needs for one person are food, clothing, and shelter. But, society is another story. Food keeps body and soul together. But love, respect, and caring make the living worthwhile. No matter how difficult it is to get along with other people, it is a requirement of our inner humanity to relate to other humans.

Living alone is good because it lets the heart expand to the point where other people can be allowed in. I wonder how many of societies' ills are caused by the lack of solitude. We get away from others to learn the importance of the tribe, and the grandeur of human relations.

There is a saying that is becoming popular today, "It takes a village to raise a child." If we take the time to look deeply into this idea we find how intricately the web of human relationship is woven into our beings. I think it takes a village to create any relationship—it takes many people to make a spot where friendship can grow and love can bloom.

Clothing keeps the body warm and gives us a certain style, but education and experience gives us a personality, a larger self to wear. Education requires lots of people paying attention. Sometimes education leads to wisdom, and then you also have dignity. These are more important things to wear than simple clothes.

I was sitting there in my meadow, surrounded by the wilderness night, with a warm jacket and new boots. I was watching my world closely, maybe for the first time in my life. My flute song sent my life out to the millions of stars overhead. I had a light-specked canvas over my head. Shelter.

Shelter keeps off the elements. Sheltering one little person all by herself is easy. But the more people you have, the more intelligence it takes, because people also require movement. Shelter and transportation bring us grace. Doing this right takes a lot of intelligence! Take a look at the traffic jams winding through any city and you'll know we haven't gotten it right yet. I had walked to my tipi, and that was the best way to go on that day. But the rest of us are being driven mad by our transportation. To really be full human beings, here and now in our modern world, we need shelter and transportation.

Back in the days when people could walk to the places they needed to go, the way I walked to my tipi, we had a feeling of belonging in our world. I felt it that night, poking my stick into my fire.

It seems to me now, that to become fully human again, we need to be fed with love, clothed with wisdom, and sheltered and transported with grace. This can't be had without a loving tribe, without a cohesive humanity. So there is the real question.

Survival used to be an individual thing—food, clothing, and shelter were enough to do the trick. But now, with over six billion people on the planet, survival has turned into a problem for society, a global thing. It's the imperative for our day.

The stars shone bright on my meadow. Up in the high mountains, with no city lights to dampen the view, the Milky Way was bright enough to swallow me. I was floating in the universe.

There is a story about Buddha. When he died he went up to the gates of heaven and all the past, enlightened masters were there to greet him and welcome him in. But he refused to enter, stubbornly standing by the gates declaring that he would not go in until every last human being had entered first. He had tasted the vast reaches of the universe and saw that all of humanity was one. He would not step through the gates of heaven by himself.

This is a poignant story to me; it means that I cannot be fully enlightened until everyone else joins. You cannot enter the gates of heaven as a solitary human being—because you are not a solitary human being. We share molecules and mind. No matter how disgracefully everybody else is living, you are still a part of it. This is why the aware person always has to reach out. This is why we have the feeling of honor.

Buddha was not the only one to see it. Sufi mystics (who are the enlightened offshoot of the Muslim religion) say that religiousness is a love affair with existence. This love affair with the vastness of existence shows us to be very small, and brings a deep humility.

The Koran says there are three basic qualities that have to be in the heart of the seeker. The first is *khushu*. *Khushu* means humbleness, ordinariness. The second is *karamat*. *Karamat* means charity, sharing—the joy of giving. And the third is *sajd*. *Sajd* means truthfulness. It is the imperative to not pretend but to be whatsoever you are, authentically. These are three pillars of the Sufis.

The first pillar—*khushu*—can be done alone. You can sit around in a tent and be ordinary (you can also sit in a tent and consider yourself to be the most extraordinary thing that ever happened), but the second and the third qualities require other people. To be sharing, *Karamat*, you must have someone to share with. It's important to be truthful to yourself, *Sajd*, but you also need others to test this truth.

Truthfulness and sharing are difficult because they also require cooperation—which is so hard to get. What if you try to give a gift and it is refused? That is the most painful thing that can happen. Very risky business! And what if you are truthful and rejected? Then you have to be like the Buddha, waiting at the doors of heaven for the others to come.

Once there was a Sufi mystic traveling through the desert with his disciple. When night came they pitched the tent and the master went inside to sleep. It was the disciple's job to tether the camel before he could rest. But the master had been teaching that day about trusting in God. So the disciple just said a little prayer, "I trust you, God, to take care of the camel," and went to sleep.

Next day they got up and found the camel gone. The master was mad. The disciple explained that he had trusted in God to take care of things. And the master answered (probably after giving that disciple a big slap), "Trust in God, but tether the camel first. God can only take care of things through *your* hands."

I had my tipi, food, fire, and new boots. For this night my hands had taken care of things: food, clothing, and shelter. My camel was tethered for the night. A little tipi in a meadow was giving me life. The soft sounds of the breeze in the trees that night eased my ears. Right now I was being alone, and that was good.

After a while the coldness of the night made the flute difficult to play. I cleaned it and put it back in its case, then I crawled into my sleeping bag, content. Stubby curled up by my neck, purring.

Chapter Four

Tipi Living

My tipi was a magic connection to the past, a time of natural people. Houses made by women, soft and sewn. A bunch of people could put them together for company. They could pack them up whenever they wanted and go. All it took, to make a life back then, were legs and hands.

I rested that night, rolled up in my sleeping bag. As I drifted off to sleep I was content. My legs and arms felt strong. My trusty boots stood guard near my head with my wire-rimmed glasses tucked safely inside. I felt in charge of my world in a way I had never felt in civilization. I could walk myself where I wanted to go. I could build my house.

I wasn't scared or lonely. In fact, I was quite pleased with myself. From my point of view, society didn't suit me. The dirty smoky cities were full of pollution, pavement, and mean people. Not for me. I had the stars, a couple of dogs, and a cat. I had no ambitions and no worries. My 500 dollars was holding out very well in my pocket with nothing to spend it on. I had some "private business to attend to."

Walking without Pockets

Along with the tipi, I had inherited a pile of garbage from the disaster last winter. Inside the pile were Bev's old books. There were a few volumes about wild edible plants and Indian herbal healing. I dried the books off in the sunshine the next day.

Armed with my new wealth of knowledge, I decided to go foraging. It was a warm sunny day, and since I was alone and such a natural, back-to-the-land person, I decided to go barefoot and naked. Like Lala, the naked dancing mystic of Cashmere, I would frolic through the woods. I had achieved a major life goal.

I stripped off my shoes and clothes, and left them in a pile in front of the tipi. Without a stitch, I headed through the meadow and up the nearby hills. The naked dogs followed along. Stubby stayed home, glaring at us with slanted eyes as we tromped across the meadow. My bare white skin, inherited from my Irish background, was glowing in the sun. The only thing I had on was my glasses.

Because of my big buildup about freedom, and women sewing tipis, and little Indian Buddha's out in the woods, you probably think this adventure opened up lightening bolts of revelations from the sky. Actually, what I discovered is that walking naked through sunny meadows is okay, but the second you get into the shade of the trees it is downright chilly, especially when there are still lumps of spring snow tucked into the deep shade. Meadow grass and soft pine needles are good for bare feet, but prickly thorny sticks and sharp rocks are another story. The chilly gushy mud in the shade squished through my toes, numbing them instantly, sucking body heat so my goose bumps grew big enough to hurt. My body was made of pins.

I made it up a small hill to the east of my clearing and found a dirty muddy pond. It was shady and cold. I wasn't having any fun. There was nothing to eat there, only kinikinic—Indian tobacco. It wasn't the sort of great time you'd expect when naked. I discovered that if you go for a hike, naked, in the Colorado mountains you don't get very far, even though it seems like a long way. And when you do get somewhere, and want to collect edible plants, you don't have any pockets.

Just a slight oversight, but I would admit no defeat. I picked myself a bunch of kinikinic and began tiptoeing back to camp with my treasure clenched in my fist. I wasn't tiptoeing to be secret—I'd cut my heel.

What a relief to break out of the trees into the sunshine! I was never so happy to see my blue jeans and T-shirt as I was that day. They had warmed in the sun. I slipped the toasty shirt over my goose bumps, feeling the warmth and comfort melt into my skin. I was becoming less ethereal by the moment.

I did learn a lot about Indian healing herbs that summer. If you smoke kinikinic it gives you a terrible cough. Yarrow helps heal coughs. In fact, half the herbs in Bev's books were about healing coughs. The other half were for healing arthritis. Some herbs dealt with other minor complaints, but mostly I had books with a hundred and one ways to heal coughs and arthritis. It was a good thing too, since my throat was raw and my joints were beginning to ache.

Meadow Basics

Willow is the best firewood when you are living in a tipi. This was a thing that Joe had reluctantly taught me (secrets are power you know; he didn't like to give them away). Sagebrush was second best. Mountain Mahogany was also a fine choice, but grew in such limited areas that it was not an option. Pine and other softwoods were last-ditch choices.

Willow is easy to overlook as firewood. It's really nothing more than a bush, but all those tiny branches are hard wood. When dry, it burns hot and clean. It grows fast in dense clumps; larger branches die off regularly and stay standing, propped up by the living bush so they can dry thoroughly. You don't need an axe (one less thing to carry around). Dead branches can be pulled out easily and broken to length over a blue-jeaned knee.

Short, daily forages to the local willow clumps kept me well supplied in firewood. My fires burned hot and clean, producing little smoke, and leaving only bits of ash.

Sagebrush is a harder wood than willow: in both texture and effort. It smells good and burns very clean, which means it burns with little smoke: important in tipi living. Sagebrush is less plentiful and tough to gather. This hardy plant grows in harsh areas and is not as prolific. Sagebrush grows slowly because it uses little water. It lives hardy and dies reluctantly. You don't find a lot of dead dry sagebrush. It's a fine treat when you can get it.

Hard, clean burning wood is important for healthy camping. Living in a tipi is like living in a chimney—it *is* living in a chimney. If you adjust the smoke flaps right the smoke rises pretty well, but it is still comparable to smoking a couple packs of cigarettes a day.

My cough was growing worse.

My bed, in the tipi, was pretty old fashioned. I had my sleeping bag and a few blankets thrown on the ground. This was my first experience of sleeping on the ground for an extended period of time.

Human bodies are mostly made of water. A good portion of this leaks out through the skin every night when sleeping. I didn't realize the extent of the problem until I crawled into my bed one night, about a week later, and found myself trapped in a clammy and stinky goo until the sun came up. By morning my joints were creaking and sore. I learned a quick lesson. Sunny afternoons are for airing the bedroll. No exceptions!

As I read further through my tipi book, I learned that enterprising Indians would make raised beds from willows to keep the hides dry, thus lessening their arthritis pains. They smoked yarrow to ease coughs. Hmmm.

On sunny and warm days, there was no better place to be than a tipi in a small meadow. Every morning, as soon as the sun rose over the trees to the east, I shed my clothes and practiced a yoga routine from a Hatha Yoga book. Sun on my skin, and a nice soft blanket let me know I was thoroughly alive. It probably helped un-stink me a bit too. The water in the creek was too cold for swimming.

I continued with my walks, well clothed and shoed now, and slowly learned the plants around my home. Yarrow was easy to find, with its feathery leaves, it was scattered throughout the meadow grass. Horsetail grew down by the stream bank. There was a patch of False Solomon's seal at the south edge of the clearing. I thought I found some wild onions, but was afraid to eat them because my book warned that this variety looks a lot like Death Camas. The illustrations weren't good enough for identification to risk something called, "Death Camas."

I poured through my books, propped against the warm, leaning-rock by my outside fire pit. I loved to lie there, soaking in the early morning sun, and reading about natural "cures" for arthritis and coughs. After awhile I started to catch on: wouldn't it be better to *not* live in a chimney, and to sleep in a dry bed, then to spend your life "curing" yourself from coughs and rheumatism? Hmmm.

Food

The best way to cook when living in a tipi in a meadow is in a fire pit. I dug a nice sized hole out by my leaning-rock. Every morning I started a lively fire. The flames transformed my willow wood into a fine bed of coals. Trial and error was my cookbook.

Daily, after breakfast, I stuck a pot with beans, rice or lentils, and plenty of water down inside the coals and covered it with a heap of ash. Sometimes, I would have a burnt mess, or uncooked goo, when I dug it out later in the evening. But most of the time I would come home to a nice, hot, slow-cooked meal. My meals were flavored with dried herbs and bits of things I had gathered. I used my wild foods carefully, getting used to them. I had a little cheese with me, and some crackers. Breakfast was oatmeal or granola with dried milk. That was it. I had to carry all my food in four miles. Dried food was the only thing that qualified as light enough.

One time I tried making my morning oatmeal in the fire pit. I stuck the pot under the coals of my night fire before going to bed. It was great to get up and have some nice hot oatmeal. But in the long run I decided the advance preparation was too much trouble. I had to get it together at night when I was tired. I couldn't crawl into bed, still warm from the fire, and watch through the open flap of my tipi door as the flames burnt down. Instead I had to sit up, shivering, as the last pieces of wood burnt down into coals, then dig out a hole and bury my breakfast. All that work created no discernible difference in the taste of the oatmeal. Why bother?

Meadow Friends

I had my tipi arranged according to the good-Indian housekeeping tips from my tipi book. My bedroll was along the sloping backside, fire ring towards the front, stores of food, and my little pots and books to each side. These arrangements quickly introduced me to the other occupants of my meadow.

Mice challenged my rice stores, thus instigating my life-long search for perfect food containers. At that time, with lesser means, I discovered that spreading things out, so the mice couldn't hide, enabled my pets to keep the rodents in check.

Sheela was a superb mouse catcher—better than the cat. To catch her prize she would freeze over a clump of grass, ears pricked, eyes bright; stand there for the longest time, not moving; then suddenly pounce and come up chewing. Saved me on dog food. In later years, I worked in an apple orchard and the owner wanted to hire Sheela full time as a mouse control officer.

Later still, when I moved to the lowlands, I found her to be a fine rattlesnake catcher. She would freeze; then pounce, grab the monsters in the middle and shake them quickly, flipping from side to side, breaking the spine. Then she would drop her catch on the ground, and methodically bite the long bodies from top to bottom, crunching each bone until the snake stopped wiggling. A horrible thing to watch, but it kept the yard safe.

Stubby the cat was less spectacular in her hunting. She liked to stay to herself, be fed and occasionally offer herself up for a pet. She caught her mice silently and without a lot of fuss. Cats are that way.

But dogs love company. My two companions protected me and kept by my side till I began to think like a dog. To this day I can hear things that other people don't notice. I learned to pick up the slightest change in the meadow sounds. Well, not sounds. If you really learn to listen it is not actual sounds that you pick up first, but a slight change in ear pressure that lets you know a sound is coming. I still do it just like a dog or a deer. Something will change in the tone around me and I'm immediately curious. I lift my head, cocking ears in the direction the change came from. Then, in a bit, I hear the sound and decide what it is.

With right hearing I learned to know if a car was over on the road, or if a plane was coming from far off, or if little doggy pads were making footprints around my tipi. To hear three dimensionally you have to first know exactly where you are. The tone of your world becomes so familiar. Then, at the first slight change of that tone, you notice, head lifts, ears prick.

This is why noise pollution in a city is so damaging to people. We are wilder, more natural than we think. Too much noise and people become blind in their ears. The world gets smaller. When people are not able to hear the tone of their world they have a hard time harmonizing.

In my meadow I had three dimensional hearing and roving sentries. My dogs watched for me and knew the movements of the meadow day and night. I got so I could tell by the twick of their ears, or the tone of a bark, exactly what type of animal they were inspecting. I lived in a three dimensional world. Very ripe and alive.

At night, Levi, being part coyote, invited the wild ones to surround the meadow and sing. I think she would have invited them right into camp if she could have. But Sheela would not allow that. She gave the pack strict instructions that they were never to come too close. Together they would join in the nightly singing. Levi with her high, wavering yips, and Sheela with a low, musical yowell. Sometimes I would join too. Why not enjoy the party?

Getting There

I lived in total contentment for about a month until I found my food supplies dwindling, and my appetite for something else growing. One morning, I gathered my two dogs, and Stubby the cat, and we headed for Leadville. I suddenly had a hankering to see old friends. I grabbed my pack, and crawled across the log towards civilization. The dogs followed willingly; the cat occasionally needed a lift. We hiked four miles out the Homestake Creek road to the highway and caught a ride to town.

Digression time.

As I write this book, I'm trying to find some way to keep from disclosing my method of transportation in those days, but I can't avoid it any longer. I did not own a car. Freedom from the automobile was one of the things that enabled me to live the lifestyle I choose.

Remember my transportation and shelter theory? These things can make our survival graceful. Unfortunately, in our modern world, the cost of transportation and shelter makes us slaves—not to mention the fact that environmentally these things are killing us. Cars are expensive and dirty, any way you want to look at it. To pay for a car you have to have a job. To have a job you have to have a car. You also have to live where everybody else lives and eat their dust and smoke. It is one of those viscous circles of life that I've always rebelled against.

I didn't have a car. I would hitchhike. Occasionally I might borrow a car. Most the time I would go out, stand on the road, stick out my thumb, and see who would take me there. I had my dogs for protection and I had a certain amount of luck leading.

It was a crazy thing for a person to do then, especially a girl. I had a few close calls with some creeps. Part of what kept me safe was my blazon belief that I was a full human, not some weak, helpless "girl."

There is an attitude that can protect a person from being a victim. This doesn't mean that if you have been hurt it is your fault. In fact it is exactly the opposite. Having the right attitude at the right moment is strictly an accident. It can't be manufactured by affirmations, or created in any way.

Some of my car rides were less than enjoyable. One driver, I remember, insisted he was taking a "short cut" and drove off down a country road. When it finally got through my thick skull that this guy was planning on using me as a helpless female (me!), I got so angry that I ended up scaring him more than he scared me. He let me out by the side of the road and I hiked back to the highway.

My reaction wasn't a manufactured response put on to manipulate my attacker. It was total—an instant outrage. I was saved by my own nuttiness.

Once, when I lived in Leadville, I was walking home late at night. I noticed this one guy following me, about half a block back, stalking. Each time I looked behind he would slip behind a building, like I couldn't see him or something. Finally I did a sudden about face, and confronted him.

"What are you doing?" I demanded.

"I'm going to follow you home." he sneered.

I noticed a car of four guys ahead of me and decided to get some help. So I ran up and said, "Hey you guys, I'm being followed by some creep. Could you help me?" The skulking figure disappeared into the shadows.

One of the guys got out of the car and replied, "Sure. We'll get rid of him and keep you for ourselves." All four joined in laughter. That was really funny. Yeah.

The red came out of my head, I bet I gained two feet and a hundred pounds in one breath. My hair stood up, making me even larger. I let them have it. The tires on their *car* wilted!

Stomping away, I kicked a telephone pole as hard as I could. The bolt of pain shooting through my toes helped to clear my head. As I marched up the hill towards my house, I noticed the shadow-man reappear behind me. I turned and pointed, ordering him away with a command you'd give to a cowering dog. He skulked off and I stormed home. So much for gallantry! But I learned a valuable lesson—after you get saved, who is going to save you from the saviors?

I don't know how a person can manufacture a rage that actually makes you grow. So don't blame yourself if you haven't stood up to the bullies in your life. I'm more stupid than the average person and stupidity can sometimes lead to moments of grace. If you don't feel the victim, you're less likely to become one. But that feeling requires the accident of being free of victimization. Don't push it.

Now, years later, I've had my share of hurts and harm. I tend to cower more when confronted. In compensation I've gained a little wisdom in staying out of harm's way. But all in all, truth be told, I think it's mostly luck. Hither and thither come the winds of experience. Sometimes you can ride the winds of change, sometimes you're just blown away. Either way, it's probably not a good idea to hitchhike.

My wildness has led me to some roads, and my reluctance has led to others. Seems like whatever passion grips me in the moment is the thing that leads to more wonder. I've had those moments of success and freedom—all those positive things we believe should be the only side of life: laughter, pride, sunshine, and love. Other times it is the dark hurt, loneliness, and even death that leads me to a new space. I'm not sure if I'd trade one for the other.

There is an old Chinese saying: "Wise man falls in the ditch once." Caution is a wonderful thing: it keeps you from falling in the giant pits that are dug on the side of the road. But sometimes, maybe only occasionally, it is a good thing to put on the blinders and blunder forward on the crooked path with no bulbs lighting the way. That's how you find new things.

So, with that tirade behind me, I can now say: I hiked out the Homestake Creek road to the highway, stuck out my thumb, and caught a ride into Leadville. Once in town I dropped by some friends' house, and was enthusiastically given a piece of floor to make my bed and home for a few nights. I was offered a bathtub and a fresh, hot meal. Oh boy!

Even with dogs and cat in tow, I was welcomed in. I had become a curiosity. Those who were sticking to their jobs and paychecks were eager to share their space with me, and I was eager to share my experience with them. They were going to have a hard time following me, as I was soon to discover.

Chapter Five

How a Cabin Finds You

The Mouth Can't Go as Fast as the Brain Can

The mind is a strange thing. We rarely get a chance to see it because we are too busy being led around by it. But if a person does something weird to their daily habit pattern, *poof*, the mind shows itself for the little monkey it is. Weeks by myself had set my brain into a new orbit. With no daily conversations or outside stimulus it had shifted into high gear, filling in the gaps. The change had come upon me gradually, so I hadn't noticed. It was happening in my mind, after all. Invisible.

Day by day, in my meadow, I was busy with those everyday activities of life: gathering wood, fetching water, cooking rice, exploring the mountains, yoga postures in the early morning sun. My mind had nothing else to do, so it recorded and analyzed each little thing I did. It's a constant yipping thing, the mind: asking questions, coming up with answers, sucking up information from every source.

Interacting regularly with other people keeps the mind in check—to the point where you hardly even notice the thing. Stimulus is a cover-up. A thought comes in, and you express it. The other person responds. Then you respond back and everything goes along nicely, what we call "normally."

Daily routines: getting up, going to work, telephone calls, washing the dishes, talking with friends, going to a party: all these things keep the mind at a familiar and unnoticeable hum—so familiar it is hypnotizing, invisible. You can only see the mind as a foreign creature in your head when it goes strange. Eastern mystics love this stuff. I didn't have a clue so it came to me unexpectedly.

Living alone in my tipi I had inadvertently created a mind-blowing situation for myself. With no music, TV, or other mental occupation, my mind started going in its own direction without interruption. I didn't notice that I had started flicking from subject to subject with turbo speed, following my own chain of thoughts.

It all made sense to me because I was there. Anyone else, listening in, would have known I'd gone whacko. For instance: say I needed a bucket of water from down at the creek. Here's how my brain might rattle along:

I start looking for my bucket, which reminds me that I had almost forgotten my pocket knife at the creek yesterday; and that my pocket knife was getting awfully dull, so maybe I should try to get a sharpening stone someplace; but would it be possible to find a rock which could do the same thing? What did the Indians do? I should learn to use all natural things, especially if I wanted to go totally native, not to discount the fact that I'd never sharpened a knife before in my life. I remembered my grandfather sharpening his knives 'till they had a rounded curve, my grandmother wrote me letters all the time. Often they had a five-dollar bill enclosed. I got my mail at Barb's house. Barb could always pick out a great bottle of wine, but maybe it would be better to save my money for food. I'm getting low on lentils. I wonder if split peas are as nutritious as lentils. How do you find out? Does splitting them do anything to the vitamins?...

As my hand was still reaching for the bucket, my mind raced from water to split peas in a logical stream of events. I knew what it all meant, but who else in the world would ever be able to figure out where the lentils came from? This was going to cause difficulties in conversations.

Flash forward to me in town on my first visit since going wild. I went to a party. I remember meeting a guy named Bob.

"Hi, there, what's your name?"

"Bob."

"What do you do, Bob?"

"Got a job up at Blackcloud mine."

"I used to work there." *Pictures of working at the mine flash through my head, remembering one nice guy who had taught me how to shovel using my leg as a brace.* "Is Randy what's-his-name still working there?"

"I think he works up in the Mill," says Bob. "I'm underground. What job did you have?"

"I worked in the mill, mixing the chemicals." And I'm thinking, *that had been an awful job. I was covered with green chemical slime day and night, probably ten kinds of cancer are growing in me right now—but it had given me enough money to move to the tipi. Still have lots of money left—enough to go to Denver for some more supplies.*

Out of my mouth, "The bus goes to Denver." In my head: *maybe I could buy food in bulk at a health food store in Denver instead of buying groceries here in town; macrobiotic health people say that when you live in a cold climate you should eat short grain brown rice instead of long.* "Have you tried the short grain brown rice?"

"I don't know."

Not only am I talking crazy, I'm talking fast, because my thoughts are going fast. Even while he was answering my last question my mind raced on. I hadn't spoken a word in weeks, and now it was a flood bursting from my mouth. *Seaweed is good in rice; trick is to add the seaweed before the rice so it doesn't clump up. Seaweed is also very easy to carry to the tipi—when dry it doesn't weigh much. Like those porcupine quills Barb gave me.*

"Porcupine quills are hollow."

Maybe I would make some jewelry or sew something neat. Gotta remember to get needles and thread before heading back to camp; pretty soon I will need to patch the knees of my pants.

I say, "and I can patch pants to make them last forever," my words tumbling over each other trying to keep up with what's going on in my head. Thinking...*Patching is better for preserving pants than not washing, in fact. I had stopped at the Laundromat on my way into town, and they'd raised the prices on the machines, I'd rather spend the money on some cheese; maybe I should buy myself some bread.*

Before drawing the next breath I say, "They have whole wheat bread at the grocery store now."

Bob was quiet, staring at me while a month of repressed talking streamed from my lips. I'd completely forgotten that he could only follow what comes out of my mouth, not what goes through my head. I sucked in a breath, fuel for more words.

Thinking...*The bread would probably get squished in my pack, unless I left all the washed clothes out, but then I'd be running around naked—of course that's pretty cold. Streaking had just become a big thing, people ripping off their clothes and running through public places as protest.*

"Did you hear about that guy who streaked the president?"

Suddenly I noticed the face of my victim. Bob was frozen with fear. The look stopped me. Like a bell ringing in a Tibetan monastery, I had a Zen "stop" meditation. The party froze around me; time stood still. I saw nothing but Bob's round eyes, the pupils wide and black. I was drawn down into them, into the fear. He was afraid of *me!* That look split me in two as I realized he had only been party to a fraction of my conversation. The rest had sped through my mind like a steam engine—and it was all nuts. I saw my own mind for the first time in my life.

Weird.

There was me, the one who should have been in charge, and there was the mind—which had been raging out of control. All in a split second. My mind continued to float in its own direction, an entity of its own. But I caught hold of it, like a wild creature in my head. I attached a note of warning—watch this thing that it doesn't run wild in company.

Too late for Bob. He turned tail and fled.

Zen meditators struggle for years to get a glimpse of the unrelated mind. I can see how it would be a difficult thing to find if you were looking for it. Better to be an unwitting dope living in a tipi. Then it comes looking for you.

I shut my yap and focused on the party; no sense in scaring more people. Through the rest of the evening I kept the observer turned on to make sure I didn't alienate anyone else. Slow down. Slow down. I found that if I concentrated I could talk coherently. If I *really* concentrated I could listen to people. My popularity rose. The party continued.

Home Again

All in all, I found visiting in town to be pretty exhausting. One night and one party were about all I could take. Next morning I felt the urge for escape. The dogs woke me up as the sun rose. I packed my sleeping bag, and let myself out the door while my hosts were still sleeping. It was a two-mile hike to the grocery store on the edge of town.

I put my pack outside the sliding front door and gave it a firm and commanding pat, which summoned the attention of my pets. "Stay." Levi and Sheela wagged their tails with a willing "Yes" to my command. I set Stubby on top of the pack. She gave me a defiant look. "I'll stay if I want!"

Inside, I bought some cheese, crackers, and fruit (no bread). I came out and found my family waiting patiently, even Stubby. They followed me eagerly to the highway, where I caught a ride to the Homestake Creek road turnoff. I shouldered my pack and began the four-mile trek into my wilderness home.

Hiking is not a natural occupation for a cat, but Stubby was learning to keep up pretty well. She went in spurts, hiding by the side of the road, waiting till we were some distance ahead and then darting past us until she found another good place to hide.

The sun shone with a sharp brightness. A perfect spring day, not a cloud. Above us was a crystal blue sky, the thin air of the high mountains letting the full impact of the sun through with all its burning might. I had taken off my long sleeved shirt, tied it around my waist, and was hiking in T-shirt and jeans. The sun burned on my skin even as the high altitude breeze blew cool.

Yellow Pines grew tall by the side of the road. Their spring needles lush and green, shining. I recall the silence as my legs carried me, footprint by footprint, down the Homestake Creek road. I inhaled the moistness of the cool spring breeze, the forest aroma.

There I was, pretty new boots and patched blue jeans. Long black braids and wire rimmed glasses. One strong leg moving in front of the other, my food carried on my back, dogs about my ankles, breathing air from the plants of the earth, learning to hear with my elbows.

My feet kicked up little clouds of dust as I stepped.

I had a pretty heavy load. About half way to camp I needed a break. I let my pack to the ground and settled up in the shade against a tree. I sat silently, smelling the fresh air and listening to the wind in the trees. There is a perfume in a high forest: a mix of pine, water, and thin air. I drank with my nose and felt peace. The dogs sat near my feet. Stubby was hiding in the bushes next to the road, a few feet ahead of us.

The tone of the forest changed. I picked it up first on the outer edge of my arms and cocked up my ear. Levi and Sheela were both looking, ears up. The tone turned into the sound of an engine. We watched.

A pickup came driving up the road, so slowly it wasn't kicking dust. It passed by me and came to a stop in front of Stubby's hiding place. A tiny old man stepped from the truck and started calling in a shaky voice, "Kitty? Kitty? What are you doing here, kitty?" He was that peculiar shape that some old men get, thin legs sprouting out of a round, tree-trunk-like body. He was stooped at the shoulders, a misshapen dirty hat plastered to his head, a three-day growth of gray whiskers quilling out of his chin. I watched in amazement. Stubby strode from her hiding place and started rubbing back and forth across the man's ankles, her teeny tail pointed straight up, as high as it could.

Humph. Cats aren't supposed to like strangers.

I stood up and walked over to the old guy, suspicious.

"That's my cat."

He looked up in surprise. "Where did you come from?"

This old guy had driven right past me and my shiny boots, my pack, and my two dogs without seeing us. Yet, he had seen a little cat hiding in the bushes. This was a guy who really liked cats, and this was my introduction to Ray Kelley.

Ray, it turned out, had met Bev and Joe last fall. He thought they were crazy to live in a tipi in the winter. He also thought I was crazy, and told me so.

"What's a little girl like you doing out here?" he asked, cocking his head to the side with curiosity, trying to figure it out. I was a little girl to him even though I topped him by a good three inches.

I tried to explain. Ray knew the location of the tipi. "Come on. I'll give you a ride. You can't be out here walking." He picked Stubby up and put her in the cab. I hoisted my pack into the back of the truck, then patted the side of the bed. Levi and Sheela jumped in. I climbed into the cab with Ray and we headed off down the road, rolling slowly along, kicking up no dust. Stubby sat between us, eyeing Ray, then eyeing me. She was obviously thinking that maybe this guy could offer her a better deal.

Ray drove us to the place where the log crossed the creek.

"You can't stay here," he said, shaking his head. He tisked his tongue softly several times. "You can't go across that log, a little girl like you." He had never seen such a thing before. He told me about the mining claim where he lived, a half-mile further up the road. If I weren't crazy I would go there. He had little cabins he had built himself. They had stoves in them and everything.

I remained suspicious and declined. I was tired. I wanted to go home. Tipis are just fine, I assured him. I'd been there a month and was still alive.

He "tisked" again and shook his head.

I slapped my leg twice. The dogs jumped from the truck, tongues hanging out of their mouths in happiness. I hitched the pack over my shoulders, and tucked my reluctant cat under my arm. The log was a short jump down from the road. Levi and Sheela trotted across. I set Stubby on the log and she followed her doggie companions. Now I was being watched. Again, I considered trying to walk the log, hitching my pack from side to side to test the weight. The rushing water below changed my mind—too far; the log was too thin. I wasn't balanced or brave enough. I bent my knees to the mossy surface, gripping the familiar short branches solidly with my hands, and began my journey across. The pack bounced against my crawling back.

Ray watched, and I could feel his stress while I crawled, inch by inch. I grabbed old roots on the far side and pulled myself up the bank, waved to the person I hadn't yet pegged as friend or enemy, and turned to climb the hill to the meadow. The dogs trotted ahead. Stubby was tucked, again, under my arm, still eyeing Ray, her green eyes glowering. She was obviously weighing her options.

The next morning I was finishing my oatmeal, soaking up sun in front of the tipi, when a strange sound broke the stillness. It came from the creek, down by the log. Very faint, but I could hear it. A whistle blowing. It blew and blew. A pause. What was happening? Again, nothing but the wind moving the trees. I twitched my ears in the direction the sound had come. So did the dogs. Sheela sat up and smiled with her tongue. The whistle blew again, and again. It blew, now, with a determination that let me know it wasn't going to stop until I answered.

I had no choice. I walked down to the log and there, across the stream, was Ray Kelley waving his hands and a cardboard box. "Coni! Coni!" He called. "I got strawberries! Come have strawberries!"

How could I say no to fresh strawberries? I crawled across my log (easier without a pack, and feeling a little less klutzy about not walking it since a hardened woodsman like Ray Kelley refused to even try to cross it) and ate strawberries with Ray. He had gotten up early that morning and driven all the way to Vail to buy strawberries for me. This was definitely not an enemy. This was a friend and the key to a new and different future.

I stayed in my tipi that summer, occasionally answering the whistle and eating strawberries with Ray. Eventually, I went up and saw his mining claim where he had built a little city of cabins. He drove me to Vail for groceries a few times, and lent me his truck for a visit to Leadville. He never did learn to call me Connie, he always said Coni, with a long O.

When it started getting cold Ray came and moved me into one of his log cabins. His obvious stress lessened as soon as I was safely tucked away into a proper home. Little girls should NOT be living in tipis in the winter. One summer was more than enough for him. There was no arguing with him on this point.

Chapter Six

The Claim

Ray's cabins were built on a mining claim he had staked himself. He was born in 1902 and grew up an orphan. His earliest memory was standing in his crib and seeing some sort of a fire. He always wondered if maybe that fire was the thing that made him an orphan. He never knew.

Ray was raised by a family that, he believed, got him so they had someone to do the chores around a farm. They worked him hard. He didn't finish school but left his adopted home and got a job working on the railroad as a laborer. He loved the trains. On his summer vacations he hiked the mountains of Colorado prospecting for gold. That must have been in the 1920s and 30s. During those days he met the real old-timer gold prospectors who had been young men searching for gold in the gold rush. They showed him how to stake out a mining claim, blast big holes into the mountains, and build little cabins. He staked out a claim for himself and did his own blasting with gusto during his vacations from the railroad.

When he retired from the railroad he was given a fine watch and bought himself a farm. Farming didn't turn out to be his style so he sold it (the farm, not the watch) and retired onto his mining claim. By the time I met him he was 72 and had been living on the claim, full time, for over a decade. The watch still kept perfect time.

Ray Kelley had three mining claims staked out in the national forest on Homestake Creek and had built his own little town of cabins by hand. Four cabins were at the top end of a meadow, about a half-mile off the road, and one was hidden in a grove up the steep hills to the west. That one was called the upper claim.

The cabins were little hobbit houses. They were six feet tall at the highest point. The doors were short, just tall enough for Ray to walk through, about five and a half feet. I had to duck to get in. Bunk beds were built into one end. Or perhaps I should say the cabins were built around a set of bunkbeds, since each cabin was exactly as wide as a bed is long, and the beds were actually part of the structure of the walls. Each cabin had two little windows.

Ray built his cabins from lodge pole logs stacked on top of each other and hitched at the corners. Roofs were shingled. There was no caulking between the logs. Ray had stuffed old rags into the spaces, wedging them in with a quartered, three-inch round of firewood. Each little piece of wood was tacked in with two nails. Basically, we were caulked with firewood wedges and Ray's old laundry. We had plenty of fresh air inside.

The little cabins were furnished with sheepherder stoves for heat and cooking. These were tiny wood cook stoves, about thigh high, and two-foot square. The firebox was on the left side, most of the space taken up by the little oven to the right. Two round plates on the top left side could be lifted for stoking the fire. There was a little door in front that opened for sticking longer pieces of wood directly into the firebox. Inside this door also revealed a rectangular tin for catching (and emptying ashes). The chimney pipe went straight up through the pointed, highest part of the roof.

Ray told me about some hunters, once, who had tried to start a fire in the oven! He shook his head and clicked his tongue in total disbelief. Maybe they put the fire in the oven because it was the biggest box. You'd think they would have looked for the dirtiest, blackest, burnt box. They were quickly smoked out of the cabin and qualified in Ray's mind as some of the stupidest people he'd ever seen—even with their college education! I too would discover that visitors needed to be taken care of very carefully.

Ray's handmade town had three little cabins. There was also a big cabin with two actual rooms, a high ceiling, and a full-sized door. We called it, "The Big Cabin." It was tops in luxury. Each room had windows and ceilings that a tall man could stand under. A full-size wood cook stove heated this cabin. This was Ray's masterpiece, though he considered it rather an extravagance (tisking his tongue and shaking his head to the side, as he showed me its secret luxuries). The big cabin was built special for a doctor friend of his from Denver who supposedly came up regularly for vacation. I hoped this guy would never show. I wasn't looking for such company.

Ray's claim was a half-mile off the Homestake Creek Road. We were just a bit further up the main road from the spot where I had crossed the creek all summer to my tipi. His driveway angled to the right off the road, past an open-gated fence with hand painted signs that read, "No Trespassing! Mining Claim. Danger! Keep Out!" The driveway then traveled through a small grove of trees, up to the garage, which was made of stacked lodge pole pines. This garage had three stalls making it three times bigger than our small houses. It was an open-door building that tilted somewhat to the side, and had quite a few holes in the roof. But it was good enough to hold Ray's truck and compressor (a large, rusty thing on wheels).

To the left of the garage was the Big Cabin. From there a trail led up a slight hill to my cabin on the left, down and over the spring. Just across the spring was a fork. You could go right, past a second little cabin, and then on to Ray's cabin; or you could go straight up to the woodpile and woodshed. There were two outhouses, one between Ray's cabin and the woodshed, the other down in the gully between the big cabin and mine.

Ray's cabins were built on the west side of a large meadow, up near the trees, but not in them. You could look across the meadow and see the Homestake Creek road and trees lining the creek. And up, beyond, were the massive mountains sloping up towards the Continental Divide. This was the direction the sun came to warm us in the morning, a very important thing.

Ray had a beautiful underground spring on his claim, the envy of the old-timer prospectors who used to live out here. Though Ray was very proud of the "iron dike," (a ridge of rocks that ran through his claim and was a sure sign of hidden riches), I suspect he really picked his site for the sunshine and water. His home was nothing like the foolishness of summer visitors. He would constantly point out cabins built under the trees. What a ridiculous thing to do! A sure sign of being nothing but summer folk. Obviously, these people knew nothing about winter and cold mornings. So remember, always build a cabin on the sunny edge of the trees. And really, wasn't this the same lesson Bev and Joe had learned in their tipi?

The other important lesson is to look for good water. Ray walked Homestake Creek for years before deciding on his location. He camped many places up and down the creek and eventually found his stream by digging down through a clump of grass that stayed thick and green through the dry part of the summer. He reasoned that there was bound to be water there, and he was right.

To get water flowing Ray dug a deep hole, built a crude box and inserted a long pipe. The water burbled from the ground into the box, and then ran into the pipe. This water ran fresh and clean all year round. Cold weather or drought never stopped Rays' beautiful spring. It was perfectly fresh and sweet because it filtered from the rocks inside the mountain. It tasted like candy. We thought so, at least. It was better than any creek water you could hope to find because it was pure, from under the mountain.

Old Man Harris, who had a claim up the road, was jealous of Ray's water till the day he died. Ray showed me the remains of Old Man Harris's house one day. He didn't have a good spot at all. He was in the shade and froze all winter, and he had to travel for water. Ray and I gloated over our good luck. I never did find out if Old Man Harris actually found any mineral on his claim…but I suppose that's secondary to good water.

Our wonderful water ran through its pipe and splashed into a small pool by the path, where Ray had installed a culvert. From there it flowed into a green gully, past a few big pines, and disappeared into the grass of the meadow. Down in the gully, in the shade of the pines, and near the cool water, Ray built a "refrigerator." This was a box with long legs and a sloping roof. The front, the door, and the bottom were covered with chicken wire. It had lots of ventilation and the coolness from the stream kept the food inside fresh.

Inside this wonderful refrigerator was the donut stash. I'm not sure, even to this day, why the donuts needed to be kept cool in this fashion, but there they were. And I must point out that because the spring ran by my cabin, and the cooler was over the spring, and the donuts were in the cooler—the donuts were right by my cabin. This would create certain difficulties for me (both mental and physical) during the long winter to come.

Underground water is not like creek water. It does not freeze in the bucket during the winter. The ground insulates it from the cold, keeping it a warm 45 degrees. In fact, underground spring water will melt snow where it flows, no matter how cold it gets. You can get a bucketful on the coldest day and it stays nice and wet all the way back to the cabin.

This was luxury (which was probably why Bev and Joe never moved to Ray's claim, even though they were invited). To get water all I had to do was walk a dozen steps, hold a bucket under the pipe and carry it back to the cabin. It was sweet and fresh. Tastier than creek water and a million times better than any can of soda pop you can buy in a store. Ray's creek turned me into a water addict. To this day I'll pass up a drink of anything else for a taste of good pure water. There is nothing like the feel of one hundred percent water hitting a thirsty throat. Mmmm. That's what we were made for.

Ray put me in the hill cabin because it was mostly empty. I had a new sleeping bag for the winter. It was goose down and rated to 40 degrees below zero—a combo gift from my parents and grandparents. They were smart to give me that. It kept me alive. I put my sleeping bag on the bed, arranged my bags of rice and lentils on the shelf, set out the dogs' food bowls, and I was moved in.

Ray's cabin was identical to mine, but much more lived-in. It was black from years of wood smoke and cooking. It was also older, the first one he had built. Ray's cabin was the farthest to the west. The mountain, with its great iron dike, rose up behind him. He lived there with his two giant cats, Gary and Cherry.

The cabin between us (number two) was Dick Fishback's cabin. It was really Ray's cabin, but he had given it to Dick, like he had given the hill cabin to me. Dick was an old hunter who would come up every few months, lie around in the cabin, get drunk, and then head back to Denver. He had met Ray years ago while hunting in the area. I guess his hunting days were over by the time I met him. I never saw him really walk.

The big cabin was for the big guests. This was the mysterious doctor. He was a friend of Dick's and had been introduced to the claim years ago. He had paid for all the fancy stuff needed to build the big cabin—stuff like windows, lumber, and roofing. He had some sort of connection with the Colorado Mountain Club, whatever that was. I didn't yet know.

By the time I had moved into my cabin winter was on its way. The sun was slanting towards the south and we had had a few small snowstorms. I learned from Ray that we could expect to be snowed in six months, a long time. I also learned that I had been neglectful in preparing myself for the time to come. Like the story of the ant and the grasshopper. Ray was the ant—he was ready for winter. I was the grasshopper—I'd done nothing but play my flute by my tipi. Good thing Ray was willing to help out.

Cabin Firewood

In Ray's life, spring, summer, and fall were for bringing in firewood. Winter was for burning firewood.

Now, I am sure Ray could have gotten firewood more efficiently. I'm sure he knew it too. But the overview of the thing, the gestalt, was that Ray's life was a circular whole. Getting firewood was his meditation and his exercise.

Through the warm months Ray would hike, every day, up the hills behind the cabins and carry down "sticks" of wood. These sticks were dead and dry aspen logs, usually about ten feet long and six to eight inches wide. He had a path that went up to the best grove; he would carry back two sticks at a time, one over each shoulder.

Quaking Aspen, "quakies" as Ray would call them, is wonderful wood for a cabin. Quakie is a white wood, relatively soft and light to carry when dry. It won't burn at all when it is wet. Don't even try it unless you want to get smoked out of your cabin. A Quakie must be totally dry to catch fire, but if properly dried, it burns quick and clean.

Pinewood, on the other hand, has a sap that is actually flammable. Although a wet pine does not burn very well, it will still go if hot enough. Really sappy pinewood will flare like gasoline. It makes lots of creosote in the chimney.

These are important considerations for a winter on Homestake Creek.

A good dead, dry, Quakie is easy to spot. The twigs and the bark fall off and the shaft stands straight and tall, shiny and white. Sometimes they fall over, but they often stand for years in their pristine state. The standing ones are best, of course, because they stay the driest and are well cured. You don't need an axe to get them. Just walk up and kick, they fall right over. Sling that baby over your shoulder and it's an easy walk down the trail to the woodpile. The weight of the "stick" helps your body move at a good clip.

Quakies were Ray's favorite firewood for our little stoves, and I grew to love them too. When you live in a tiny cabin that is caulked with rags and firewood, the inside temperature in the morning is the same as the outside temperature: cold. Aspen catches fire quickly and burns hot, giving a fast heat to the cabin. It also burns down completely, leaving very little ash—not like nasty pine that keeps you in a constant dither emptying the ash box.

For this first winter, however, I had not collected my share of aspen. So Ray and I hopped in his truck and headed off to the high country for a load of lodge pole pine. This was a rather blasphemous journey for Ray. We had to actually use saws (handsaws) to gather this horrible wood. And I can tell you, pine is a lot harder to saw than Quakie. The teeth of a handsaw slides through cured Quakie like butter. But pinewood grabs and chokes the saw's teeth with its sap. It took us all day to fill his truck with a nice, neat stack of perfectly straight lodge pole.

Ray was careful to stack the lodge pole by the garage, which was over near my cabin, so no one would associate him with such a thing. It was tossed unceremoniously on the ground in a flat stack. Nothing like his well designed "lean" of wood against the tree by his shed. Just my style. I was mighty pleased. We spent two days, and gathered two loads, to make sure I would have enough.

I was able to redeem myself somewhat, though. There were still quite a few warm days before the heavy snow, so I was able to join the daily ritual and carry in some extra quakies so I could get my fire hot quickly in the mornings. My quakies went in the big stack over by Ray's shed, and we shared equally.

Ray stacked his wood in a big pile, up on end and leaning against a tree near his chopping shed. This way the wood stayed dry and snow wouldn't pile on top. People from the Colorado Mountain Club would sometimes laugh at Ray because he had such a large pile of wood. Ray knew they didn't have a clue about winter in the cold. He would humph and waggle his head in front of them. Later he would inform me of their latest foolishness.

Ray had a truck, an old four-wheel drive. The big question, for the moment, was do we let the truck get snowed in with us, or park it out by the highway? If the truck got snowed in we were pretty much stuck until spring thaw.

On the other hand, leaving the truck out by the highway was risky. It would be unprotected there and subject to vandalism or theft. It could get impounded as an abandoned vehicle, and we would have to inform the Highway Department of its presence. If not impounded it could get buried by the snowplows.

The third option was to park it down by the first house on the Homestake Creek road. Ray was friends with the owners and had a key to the place. They were summer visitors only, and he occasionally kept an eye on things for them. *Why don't we look the place over?* We hopped in the truck and took a drive on down.

At the beginning of Homestake Creek the road turns off the highway and quickly goes downhill with two switchbacks through a thickly wooded area. In the summertime you drive down the road and think, *"Oh how lovely,"* because you are immediately hidden from the highway and enjoying the lovely smelling pines. In the wintertime, because of the hill, you get stuck. The first quarter mile of road was the worst. It was steep, and the shade from the trees caused the snow to pile up deep and prevented an early melt-off. There was already enough snow accumulated there to make us have to go into four-wheel drive to get up.

We drove up to the highway, parked, got out of the truck, looked around, and had a discussion about leaving the truck up there. We both clicked our tongues and shook our heads with doubt. No good.

So we hopped back into the truck, turned around, and drove back to the place at the bottom of the hill. It was a nice house with a large driveway. We parked the truck and took a walk now, back up the road toward the highway. If we parked the truck at this house, it would have to get up this hill.

I was trying to imagine this piece of road in the full of winter, gauging the slant of the trees against the winter sun. Reality was clear. If we parked at the bottom of the road we'd be snowed in most of the winter anyway. By the time this last hill was thawed, we'd be able to drive right up to Ray's mining claim.

Ray had lived quite a few winters out at Homestake Creek. He had experimented with both methods, leaving the truck in, and parking it out. He didn't mind getting snowed in, so the decision depended on me. Seemed to me, the best thing was to follow the lead of the wise. I added my vote: we would leave the truck in the garage on the mining claim. If we were gonna get snowed in, we might as well get all the way snowed in.

Ray and I relaxed now that we had made our decision. Since we were already parked in front of the fancy house we decided to have a peeking adventure. We used the key to let ourselves into the house at the bottom of the hill.

It was nice. Real rooms, gas lights, furniture, carpet. We walked through every room, slowly, in silence, not touching anything. We were the poor people from the little cabins. This was a big house, and rich—we shouldn't touch. Ray made a show of looking back and forth, checking for any damage, and qualifying himself for his caretaker position and entry into the home.

The house seemed far away to me, even though I was standing right inside it. I had been so long living in my tipi now, and in a six by ten foot cabin, that this sort of house floated in the realms of possibilities that can't be. Owning such a thing, living in such a thing was impossible.

I walked carefully, without touching. My mind was blank. How could anything be so rich? Ray was also silent. We were in the same place. No need to speak. We stood and smelled the foreignness of it all, and wondered. We didn't say a word to each other. Ray didn't even tisk his tongue.

As we left, we checked that we hadn't left any footprints. Nothing had been moved. We had looked silently without leaving a mark.

It was very important to shut the door and make sure it was locked. Ray, being the caretaker, took it upon himself to accomplish this difficult task. The owners had shown him how to operate the lock. He was in charge.

The houses where I grew up, in suburbia, had this same type of a lock on the bathroom doors. From the inside you push in the handle and turn it. Then from the outside you can't open it. Ray couldn't get it. He tried, fumbling. I showed him. He tried again. I showed him again.

It simply wouldn't do for me to lock the house, because Ray was the caretaker. Nothing needed to be said. I honored his authority. He tried the knob again and again, but always managed to untwist the lock, thus opening it, before shutting the door. Finally he concluded that something was wrong with it, and he shut the door and locked it by turning the key. To make sure everything was okay we both tried the knob several times. It was locked good and tight. Ray had accomplished his full range of caretaker duties.

I made a mental note. Ray was just over seventy years old and he could not shut a modern lock—something that was so simple to me I could lock it in my sleep. The world had changed so much in his lifetime that the simplest things had become impossible. It was only practical to believe that the world was going to change for me too. I knew, in that minute, that I had to pay close attention to things that were happening in my world, or I too would not be able to lock a house when I was seventy.

This explains some quirks about me today. I am a very back-home person. I never "do" my hair. I spin yarn and knit my own sweaters. Yet, I keep up on computer technology. If it is new, I get in and learn it and grow as it grows. I have read the manual for my VCR. I look for the best in microwave ovens and take the time to learn that (contrary to popular opinion) microwaves aren't nuclear. I want to be able to lock my house when I am an old lady.

Sometimes one needs to be the ant and not the grasshopper. Winter was coming. The wood was in. The truck was going to be parked in the garage until spring.

The other problem was, what was I going to eat?

Chapter Seven

How to Eat a Tree

By this time it was getting cold in the morning. I'm not naturally an early riser. I cuddle guiltily in my warm sleeping bag until the sun has risen enough to light the cabin, unwilling to face the cold until the last possible moment.

Finally, I jump out of bed. The cold hits bare skin under my long underwear. It's two steps to the stove, and I'm shivering. I slide the metal handle into the slot on the stove lid and lift it from its groove. My hand is shaking as I slide the lid back. Quickly, I crinkle newspaper and shove it into the sooty firebox, catching a streak of black along the outer side of my wrist. On top of the paper I arrange Quakie kindling, three layers crisscrossing each other to leave plenty of airspace for the fire to catch. I strike a wood match on the side of the stove, turn it upside down until it has a good flame, let it fall onto the paper, and slide the lid back in place.

There is a short pause. I wrap my arms around my chest to hold in some of my body warmth. A puff of smoke escapes from a crack near the stovepipe. I'm stiff from the cold as I adjust the damper on the chimney and open the lower vent to let in more air. A little tuft of ash sprinkles to the floor, telling me the ashbox needs emptying.

The fire slowly releases its heat into the frigid air of the cabin. First it has to heat the cold metal of the stove and then radiate into the air of my little cabin. I huddle close, begging for warmth. It's a good half an hour until I'm comfortable.

Brrrrrr. The day has started.

There was more than one way to start a fire in my little stove. Ray showed me his "quick fire" technique for warming a cold cabin. Squish a tin can at the edges so the front makes a spout, fill it with a little fuel oil (which is kind of like kerosene), and pour a thin stream of the flammable liquid over the baby fire as it starts. Nothing like a little flammable liquid to really get a fire going! Gotta be careful, though. If the flames are too high they will run right up the stream of gas and explode the can. I avoided this technique because the fuel oil left a burnt petroleum smell in the cabin.

I'd been in my cabin about three weeks now and was feeling right at home. On this day it had been daylight for a few hours, even though the sun was just beginning to peek over the mountains to the east. I heard a car off down the road coming up the driveway. Company. I was immediately suspicious. I slipped on my coat and ducked through the door. In order to see without being seen I hid by the corner of my cabin and peeked. I watched as a man, his wife, and their teenage son started unloading things from their car into the big cabin. Ray had told me that the big cabin was for some doctor; I had hoped they would never show up.

Ray came tromping down the trail past my cabin, smiling and saying hi to his friends.

I met them with tight-lipped suspicion. These were people from the other world, just the sort of humanity I had moved into the mountains to hide from. Such a thing wouldn't happen over at my tipi! I wanted nothing to do with these people. They were suspicious of me, too, but pretended to be nice. I felt the duplicity and it made my suspicion even deeper.

They brought donuts. As the Doctor handed his treasures to Ray— enough to fill the cooler to the top—Ray chomped his false teeth with glee.

This didn't suit me very much as I was under the belief (and still am, for that matter) that junk food and sugar are bad for your health. Ray was suffering with asthma and I thought that a good diet would help him feel better. It puzzled me that a doctor, who was supposed to be concerned with people's good health, would bring up boxes of donuts for an old man to eat. Once, later, I asked him, and he just shrugged his shoulders, saying it was the only thing Ray wanted.

Meanwhile I had to adjust to allowing a bit of society into my life. The doctor and his family belonged to a group called The Colorado Mountain Club. They were a bunch of people who lived in Denver and liked to take trips into the mountains. They had been using Ray's cabins as a free vacation spot. I was there now, taking up one of the cabins, but that didn't stop them one bit. They showed up every few months, winter or summer, took over the place for a few days, filled the cooler with donuts, and left.

It was nice to get a little company, I guess, but I always wondered what went on in these city folk' minds. If I had to name one quality about people who come from the city to visit the outdoors, it would be that they simply don't pay attention. It's amazing to me that any city person survives a nature trip. It's also amazing how many men can't chop firewood.

I remember one guy in particular who terrified me so much with his clumsy handling of the axe that I grabbed the weapon from his hands and chopped his wood for him. We were snowed in at the time and I didn't relish the idea of carrying some bloody stub of a person four miles to the road after he chopped pieces off himself. Being a basically polite person I didn't just grab the axe from his hand, instead I offered a lame excuse to get my hands on the weapon, "See, do it like this. You use the pointed side."

I never looked our visitors in the eye when I talked because I was always hoping they'd go away. I was dark and surly—on purpose. These people were invading my space. The guy that I had taken the axe from chatted amiably as I split his nightly supply. It never occurred to him to wonder where this wood had come from. He had never carried a single stick off the mountain. I chopped and scowled.

Looking back, it's amazing how cheerful he stayed against my bad attitude. Probably he thought I was some sort of "character." Surely I hadn't had a bath in quite awhile. He must have been pretty impressed by my wild appearance because he asked me, "What do you eat out here?"

I froze, axe in the air. For one second I tried to stop my tart reply, but I couldn't. I answered, "I eat what the Indians used to eat, just the bark off the trees."

I said that.

I glanced sideways at my victim. His eyes were wide with admiration and envy. He believed me! He glowed with fawning admiration, "Do you really? How did you learn to do that? I didn't know Indians ate bark. That's amazing!" To this day, I'm sure, he is telling people he once knew a girl who ate tree bark.

Once, I did eat tree bark. It was a beautiful day the next spring. I was soaking up sun after long days locked in the snow, when I suddenly got the urge to climb to the top of the mountain. I already had my boots on. Without preparing water or food or anything, I stood up, slapped my thigh to get the attention of my dogs, turned around, and started climbing the hillside. I went up, and up, and up, and never found anything resembling the top, which wasn't too surprising considering I was starting around 9000 feet and the tops of the mountains in that area of Colorado are 14,000.

Eventually, I realized there was no top for me that day. With that realization I discovered I was hungry and thirsty. Time to go home. I turned to head down and found myself looking over steep hillsides angling into a far away valley. The valley was blue from the distance. I was a tiny speck on the huge hillside I had climbed. Home was a long way and I was getting hungrier by the minute.

I headed straight down the mountain, back over my own footprints. Up this high there was plenty of deer sign (hoof tracks and moist black pellets). As I walked through a grove of Quaking Aspen trees I noticed teeth nibbles on the green, juicy bark of newly fallen trees. It was obvious the deer considered this a great snack. The more I walked, the hungrier I got, the better those nibbles looked to me. Saliva rose in my mouth. Those teeth marks looked just like the teeth marks I would leave in a juicy, hot corn-on-the-cob. Finally I decided: jeez, the deer really like that; I'll give it a try. I knelt down by a handy Aspen tree and sunk my front teeth into the soft outer green bark, scraping across the surface.

Pwew! Spit! Choke! It was awful. I spat and gagged. My knees went weak. It tasted like tree. Just like a tree smells. Awful! And now I was really in a pickle. I was hungry and thirsty—a long ways from water—and the most horrible taste ever was curling my tongue. I didn't even have spit left. I beelined for the closest draw that looked like it might contain water and followed it down, down, down until I finally found a trickle of water I could drink from. Suck-spit. Suck-spit. But no amount of drinking and spitting would rid my mouth of that awful taste. Whew. No more tree bark eating for me, thank you.

In my bizarre way of doing things I learned another life lesson. Deer really like the things they eat. I really like the things I eat. People have different tongues than deer. I was definitely not a deer. Learning what you are not is a mighty step towards self-realization.

Real Food

But this chapter is about food and getting something to eat when living in a little cabin out in the woods. Eating is a big deal when you are snowed in and 60 miles from the nearest grocery. Tree bark was not going to do the trick.

The fall nights were getting cold and long. Snow stuck to the ground after each storm. My thoughts turned to winter supplies. We were going to be snowed in. I knew it, and Ray Kelley told me exactly what would happen; final snows would get us by November, and we wouldn't get out till May. I needed to get in a winter's supply of food. But what? I had no clue what a person might need to eat through a winter. So I did what I have always done in difficult situations—I took a big guess.

What you eat is important to your well-being. This becomes even more obvious when the variety of food becomes diminished for some reason. My location and lack of funds were a limiting factor. I knew I needed to choose carefully, but had no experience.

Ray wasn't a whole lot of help to me because he stuck to a pretty standard American diet. I wanted to be innovative and healthy. He put in a supply of canned meat (those little canned sausage things and lots of canned ham). Also in his stores were some canned green beans, pork and beans, potatoes (both dry and real), cornmeal, and flour. There was also, of course, the supply of donuts in the cooler—those jelly-filled ones covered with powdered sugar are especially important to our story. White, powdery, jelly-filled donuts. My tongue still delights at the wonderful staleness of them, a tribute to modern food preservation. Those donuts could last forever. But that was not what I wanted.

I was a pure and natural human being escaping the scourges of modern man, and I swore that I did not want anything to do with sugar donuts and I also wanted nothing to do with canned Spam and pork and beans. I wanted organic, whole food. I had also become a vegetarian during my last winter in Leadville.

I was way above donuts and meat, evolved beyond such things. I wanted my food to be real, infused with the wholesome nutrients of the soil and sun. The question was: what is real food? Where do you find it? We had put in Ray's supplies by driving to Vail and shopping at the big Safeway store. For my supplies I borrowed Ray's truck and drove to Leadville. From there I took a bus down into Denver, where a high school friend let me stay at his house and drove me to an authentic health food store—the kind, in those days, that could only be found in a big city.

The city health food store was a strange and groovy place, filled with bags of spice and bins of whole foods. I spent two hours in the store, walking around, looking at the food, writing and erasing on my list, trying to guess what I might need for the winter. I was a stranger in a beautiful land as I bought 25 pound bags of rice, flour, and cornmeal, and five-pound bags of pinto beans and lentils. I got a big jar of honey and some dried fruit (I wanted more, but it was very expensive). I got some cheese, several pounds of organic butter (it would freeze and keep well outside) and a little fresh food.

I came back to the cabins, proud of my prizes. Ray thought I was nuts. I thought I was the super camper, supplied with the health food of primitive man. But as winter moved along things changed. Ray was satisfied. I went nuts.

The vegetarian thing was my answer to the world's problems. It was a well thought-out choice of lifestyle. I'd read a lot of books with very convincing details proving that human beings are not natural meat eaters and that meat clogged the human digestive system. It all had something to do with the way our teeth are shaped and the length of our intestines. (For real information on this topic read anthropologist Richard Leakey.) Aspiring vegetarians are fed with vivid pictures of our colons clogged with years of stale meat. It is easy to be convinced that monkeys and our natural ancestors only eat vegetables when you don't know any monkeys or natural ancestors.

I was also a vegetarian because of socio-political reasons. The world was (and is) filling up with people. Why feed grain to a cow and then eat the cow? It is more efficient to eat the grain directly. Spiritually, the vegetarian thing is about respect for life, or maybe it is fear of death, including fear of causing death in others.

I was mainly a vegetarian for investigative purposes. I figured that we didn't know one way or the other the true way to be a human. This was the private business I was attending to. Lots of people I knew were becoming vegetarians, and I wanted to find out what it was all about. Maybe the secret was there. I knew that I wouldn't find out about the true nature of vegetarianism unless I did it totally. Since I'm a total-type person (some call me obsessive), that was pretty easy to do.

I was a total vegetarian. No exceptions.

This chapter is about food, so let's take this vegetarian thing to its full conclusion, even though it plummets us way into the future.

I learned about being a vegetarian by doing it thoroughly. I found that being a total (picky) vegetarian did a good job of making my world smaller. I couldn't eat in restaurants. I couldn't be a guest at anyone's house unless they played along with my game.

I remember once, during my vegetarian period, my mother came up to the cabin, got me, and drove me down to Denver to visit my aunt. My aunt made her special meatballs and spaghetti. These meatballs and spaghetti are her pride. The recipe is a secret from generations of her family. They take two days to prepare. They take more than two days to prepare. They take heart and love, the heart and love of generations of family on her side who learned how to make the perfect meatballs. I was the strange niece who lived in a cabin in the woods. She was celebrating my return to the real world of the city with her lengthy preparations.

Then I showed up and wouldn't eat the meatballs. I only ate salad and was starving. I was nice about it, and she was nice about it, but I think I killed something more important to the world than a cow that day. I rejected my aunt's gift; I killed my full relationship with my aunt. We were smiling when we parted, but our relationship could have grown through our encounter if only I would have eaten the meatballs and enjoyed my family.

It wasn't so much that I had rejected the meatballs, as the fact that she had nothing to feed me, and that bothered her. Her natural human heart held the desire to feed me. In my search for naturalness I discounted her naturalness. I ate a lot of salad and we both felt bad.

Later, when I lived on Beaver Creek in Idaho, I had kids. My son, Jaime, was three when my daughter Tessa was born. Jaime was the most pure person in the whole world, according to my philosophies. I was total vegetarian the whole time I was pregnant with him. He had never eaten a piece of meat in his life. He had never eaten sugar or any processed food. He had only eaten organic food.

Tessa happened to be born a few hours after midnight, January 2nd. She was the first baby of the year born in Lemhi county. The New Year's baby gets prizes every year and our prize came from the Cow Bells, which is a club of ranch wives. It was a beef roast in the same weight as the baby. It came with a little bib that said, "I love beef." Surprise. We got our picture in the paper with a short article saying what an irony it was that the beef roast went to a vegetarian.

We didn't throw our gift out. We decided to cook it up for our guests (my family), who had come to help with the baby. I read instructions on how to cook a roast, and cooked it up good. Jaime was an innocent three-year-old. He got himself over to the table, took a taste of the roast, and went ballistic. He was a starving animal! He crammed meat down his throat like a mad man. He didn't even chew. Here was my perfectly natural kid. He loved meat! He couldn't get enough of it—his hands were shaking with his hunger. He was a wild thing and obviously a meat eater to his core, even with all his years in training to be vegetarian. From that day on the kid demanded to eat meat.

The same thing did not happen to him with sugar. He never had a taste of sugar until he was six years old and doesn't have a sweet tooth to this day.

Remember the deer and the tree bark story? Our tongues are made for what we are supposed to eat. That was the day I learned the truth of vegetarianism. Totality is the best way to learn that something is a stupid idea. We don't have to live blind in our world; we can discover, through personal experience, how we fit and how to live.

Now I eat anything. I never have to offend a generous heart that wants to feed me. My world has become bigger, a full 360 degrees of possibilities in the food department. I strive to stay away from junk food because it is obvious that grease and sugar wreak havoc on body chemistry. It's the middle way.

Chapter Eight

Breathing in the Cold

My little cabin on Homestake Creek was four miles from the highway. The dirt road up Homestake Creek was not plowed in the winter, and that means it was snowed-in. In reality, however, I wasn't really snowed-in. I had legs that went all the way down to the ground, and four miles isn't such a long ways to walk. It can be done in an hour or so. Snowed-in just means that you can't drive in.

The snow came as a silent presence. The first fall snows drifted down, sugaring the world with white. Then, snows with more intention brought ever-thickening layers. Finally, there came the "big snow," and that was the end of it.

Each time a snow came, even the tiniest spattering of white, Ray would get out his broom and sweep the trails. At first I thought he was a little nuts. He also thought I was a little nuts for not knowing that every little speck of snow had to be swept off the trails, starting with the first snows. He shook his head and clicked his tongue. The trails must be swept. We will sweep them. He was up early every morning with his broom. I was up late every morning with mine, trying to catch up.

Ray had a radio and a supply of batteries. The only time he would sit up at night was to listen to baseball games. He also had a baseball board game that he had invented. He could sit and play his board game while listening to the announcers of the real games being played hundreds of miles away. Sometimes I would sit with him and help play the game. I never really understood how it was supposed to work, but he was content to move my pieces along with his, so I never had to know the rules.

I remember one night: we were sitting up, playing the baseball game and listening to the radio. Night was the only time we could listen to the radio because radio waves travel better at night and were able to reach down into our little canyon. In the daytime all we got was static. We couldn't listen to the radio all the time anyway because that would use up the batteries. The snows were piled high and we had been snowed in for some weeks. We happened to catch a bit of news and they were saying something about President Ford. Ray and I looked at each other. "Who?"

"Do you think we missed an election?" I asked.

Ray shook his head in consternation. We were quite embarrassed with each other. You'd think we would know who the president of the United States was! For the life of us we couldn't figure out who this President Ford might be. This was still America, right? A couple weeks later, on a trip into Leadville, I asked around and found out that Vice President Agnew had resigned and Ford had became vice-president, and then President Nixon resigned and Ford became President. Who could have known! We had missed a bit of news.

Ray didn't like to go on hikes or walks in the snow. He was content to play his board game, cook his little sausages, and sweep the trails. In the years he had spent there by himself he would go out once—twice at the most—to get his mail. Taking the trip to the road was a distasteful, even frightening thought for Ray. Who knew if he would ever make it back!

I, on the other hand, liked to go places. Young and dumb, I guess. This was back in the days when cross-country skiing was just beginning to be popular. I had heard a little about cross-country skiing, but didn't have any skis. I did have snowshoes. My parents had purchased the snowshoes some years ago for a winter outing. They had only used them a few times, and had generously donated them to my wilderness experience.

For my first trip through the snow I eagerly strapped the snowshoes to my feet and headed out with immense pride. I waved to Ray as I headed away from our little cabin village. I was the great, white snowshoe walker. Things went well through the trees where the snow pileup wasn't deep or drifted. Then suddenly, Ploosh! Down I went in the snow. The snowshoes sank in the soft powder and I fell from my own momentum. I crawled forward until my feet were under me and slowly stood up. I had to stomp twice with each forward snowshoe, packing the snow before committing my weight to it. I quickly learned that snow shoes work on a fairly limited number of snow conditions. If the snow is too new, and dry and fluffy, the shoes sink down and load up with snow, adding on extra weight for legs to lift. If there is a breakable crust on top of the snow, forget it.

I never did get to like the snowshoes. The four-mile hike to the highway was a torture with my legs lifting five pounds of snow with each step. Slowly step forward, pat, pat, put my weight on the front foot, then lift the heavy shoe from behind. Shake the snow off and pat, pat again. Taking the shoes off didn't work either. I'd sink up to my thighs in the snow. I'll tell you one thing, though! I was not cold. Sweat dripped down my back as I struggled across the snow. I took off layer after layer of clothes until my wet shirt was exposed to the cold air. Whew! Ten degrees outside and it was hot!

I made it to the highway, stashed the snowshoes in the bushes and hitched to town. Then back again, out to the Homestake creek road. I strapped the monsters on my feet and began my slow hobble over the snow. I was quickly losing my interest in winter travel.

The trip back was even worse. The snow in the big meadow had developed a thick crust on top because the sun had been shining, melting the top of the snow, and then freezing up hard as evening came. It was like a three-inch sheet of glass on top of airy fluff. I could make, maybe, three steps on top of the crust, then crack! The sheet broke and the snowshoe slipped sideways into the softness underneath. Pulling my foot up was an immense effort, as I had to lift the weight of the snow that had come down with my shoe and fight against the snowshoe catching the edge of broken crust. My legs ached from the effort. I was glad to hit the trees at the bend heading towards the cabin driveway.

For Christmas time, in that first winter, my more-than-generous parents bought me a pair of skis. Suddenly, I was high styling! This was fun! The skis slid across the snow in a fast glide. Four miles of snow became my delight! As the world got colder and colder, I learned the fine art of waxing the bottoms of the skis and performing the kick step of flat cross-country skiing. I was in my element. The winter road of Homestake Creek became more delightful than the summer road.

Skiing through the meadow was the most fun. Sometimes the sky was so blue I thought I'd melted away. The cold made the air invisible. Snow-laden trees shimmered with a bright light. There was nothing but me and my own breath skiing through the meadow.

Mountaineering literature says that a person out in the mountains in the winter should always use the "buddy system." You are supposed to have someone with you in case you get in trouble. When I went places I didn't use the "buddy system" because there was no buddy. It was just me and my awareness walking through the cold.

Solitude, at 20 below zero, creates sharpness, in the air and in the mind. Things are still and silent. A little fear brings protection because it *is* dangerous. Your awareness must be as sharp as the air: you must see where each foot steps, see yourself as you walk, see the muscles that bring you forward and the dips in the snow that tell you what is below. You don't want to trip in the cold.

I think the big difference between natural man and modern man is the ability to pay attention, to see the world. We are so educated now, but our minds are in a hole. Most people think that their skin is the dividing line between what is "me" and what is the "other," so they don't really look out. Our own eyes veil our sight.

In reality, there isn't such a definite line between the inner and the outer. If you look at your skin with the eyes of physics you find yourself very porous, full of the whole universe. Breathe in and you breathe dinosaurs. Think of it. Think way, way back before there was any history of any living thing. Volcanoes made smoke which gave early plants something to breathe. The sun and the trees shared their molecules to make the oxygenated air that brought the first fish from the sea. They grew and changed together, nourished the soil with their bodies, and things grew bigger. Dinosaurs. The dinosaurs grew and filled the earth. And now, even though they are extinct, dinosaurs are everywhere. They are in the pieces of molecules in the soil that grows our food, which grows the trees, which make the air. Dinosaurs are in the oil in the ground that runs our cars, which fills our air with dinosaurs.

Did you know that stardust constantly flows down through the atmosphere, filling us with pieces of the universe? Scientists can measure how much stardust comes down each day. Every piece of rice you eat is enormous: it's filled with stardust, the people who planted it, the sunshine and winds which pushed the rain to it, the marketing executives who brought it to you. The rice goes in and fills your skin with life. All that is inside of us, is out of us too.

More than our skin is porous. Our minds are filled with vents. Mystics say that the disciple finds enlightenment in the silence between thoughts. There is a lot of silence inside the mind. Thoughts are not the impenetrable wall that they seem. They are just bits and pieces. Thoughts come from everywhere. They aren't entirely "me" or "you" either. Have you ever studied a foreign language and suddenly found yourself thinking in the new tongue? It makes you notice that you normally think in English. And where did English come from? Not from you. Not from me.

Somewhere inside the most brilliant speech made by our smartest intellectual is the first "ugh" of the first caveman. The types of thoughts that run through your head have evolved over thousands of years. They have been taught to you by your parents, teachers, friends, and a million connections to the past. Your self is full of the selves of all others. I am you. We are inextricably connected.

We are not just the group of cells under our skin, or some combination of thoughts and ideas, we are composed of infinite stardust. When we walk, we walk with the molecules of the air showering down and the whole world dancing before us. We do not own our environment, it owns us.

At 20 degrees below zero, skiing through remote Colorado tundra, you need this kind of awareness to move forward. It's not terribly dangerous, but you'd better watch. In complete solitude your worst enemy is yourself. Stupid mistakes are not easily forgiven.

Getting Cold

Extreme cold almost always has blue skies in the day—the kind of blue that stretches upward to infinity—and a million stars at night. Winter sky is deeper and wider than summer sky, so deep that any remnants of summer heat fall away from the earth. Snowstorms bring welcome warmth along with the drifting white flakes. The clouds form a protective layer over us. They lower the pressure and help the world hold its heat.

This was a weird thing for me to learn. Snow brings warmth in the winter. As a child I always thought that snow was cold. Maturity lets us know that it is the clear blue sunny days that are cold. Snowy days are warm and mild. Sometimes reality is the opposite of what the mind imagines.

I remember every step from my cabin to the road in winter, because in winter I watched every step. My step in the summer was a relaxed saunter. My step in winter was with complete knowingness.

In the Cabin

My cabin was small enough that it heated relatively quickly, but it was also porous, so the cold that ruled the outside world was completely inside by morning. I had always heard rumors that a person can stay warmer by sleeping naked in their sleeping bag. It has something to do with the skin making a pocket of warmth against the bag. This is one of those urban myths that I still hear to this day. But I have found that, for the most part, the people who tell this story are people who have never slept in a sleeping bag at forty degrees below zero. Take it from me: you'll be warmer in your sleeping bag if you snuggle in with a good pair of long underwear.

Long underwear is the key to mountain winters. The difference between a person who lives in the mountains and a person who lives in town is that the mountain person puts on long underwear in the fall, and takes them off next spring. People in town wear outfits. The purpose of clothes for a person in town is to look good.

The purpose of clothes for the mountaineer is for survival. These clothes are certainly not slimming! There are certain situations in the wilderness where you absolutely need a particular piece of clothing, and you'd better have that piece when that situation arises. Color combination is a very minor consideration.

Today there are the most amazing synthetic fibers for warmth. Back then we had good old army wool and cotton. Those old clothes didn't help a lot when getting out of bed in a cold cabin.

Getting out of bed in the morning was becoming more difficult. It was really getting cold now and I was reduced to pouring fuel oil on the fire to get it going. The cabin now felt like it had enough ventilation to disperse the fumes. My mother had given me a nice red quilted bathrobe to help keep me warm in my little cabin. I could just see her, shopping around and really thinking she'd found something when she bought this robe. Turned out that it was nothing versus the sub zero weather of Homestake Creek Colorado. A thin synthetic quilt. I would stand in my little red bathrobe huddling by the slowly growing fire. I huddled so close to the stove that I melted a hole right in the front of the bathrobe. So much for synthetics.

Ray didn't have such a hard time getting up in the morning. He didn't sleep well at night because he suffered from asthma. He would go to sleep, then wake up in the middle of the night struggling for breath. He'd get up, stoke the fire, take his medicine, and then go back to bed. His cabin never filled with the full cold of morning. He also had a lot more stuff in his cabin to hold in the heat. My cabin was bare and chilly.

My dogs lived in the cabin with me.

Ray and I faced certain difficulties with our animals. He had two giant cats, Cherry and Gary. Gary was 14 years old, and Cherry was 12. They were fat and they were old. The cats loved to snuggle up with Ray in his lap, or ride around on his shoulders. He would gently stroke them right above the ear with one bent finger, cooing little nothings at them while they purred back. Dogs were a bad thing in Ray's eyes because they might chase the cats.

"Put those dogs on a string," he would always say.

My dogs had been raised from puppies with my cat Stubby, so they weren't particularly interested in cats of any kind. I worked diligently training my dogs, and they easily accepted the fact that Cherry and Gary were the rightful owners of the Homestake Creek cabins. After a month of peaceful co-existence Ray relaxed his guard and decided that the dogs were okay—sometimes even cute.

Stubby decided, about that same time, that Ray was a more suitable cat-owner type person than me. Ray had a kitty door in his cabin so that a willful cat could come and go as she pleased. My door had to be opened by a reluctant and often lazy human. Ray's cat food always had sausage grease poured on it for an extra little zip. His cats dined on canned cat food now and again. My house only had dry nibbles. Through the winter I saw less and less of Stubby until our only contact was the stories Ray would tell me of some wonderfully cute thing she had done over at his cabin.

The dogs remained faithful. They protected me with their ears. I could tell exactly what creatures were around, man or beast, by the sound of their bark. Their coats grew thick and shiny as protection against the winter's bite. We played and slept and ate.

I can't explain what a wonderful thing it was to have nothing to do. The snow had come down and covered me with more than its white blanket of cold. It also covered me with the excuse to just sit still. Many people think that being snowed in four miles from the nearest road, and 60 from the nearest town, would be worrisome, lonesome, or even frightening. But just the opposite was true. The experience was one of absolute freedom from my own mind of worry. The wood was in and my stove was more than adequate to heat my little cabin. I had plenty of matches, newspaper, and fuel oil to start a fire. My food was stored safely in mouse-proof containers over in the corner. I had long underwear and a change of clothes, good boots, and enough wool socks to wash. Fresh delicious water ran all year round; it gushed from its pipe just outside my cabin door, danced under the trail and down to the trees until it passed (yes) the donut stash.

I was never lonely. I think the only time in my life I have ever experienced loneliness has been in a crowd, or living in town. My company was the occasional visit with Ray. The dogs provided plenty of snuggles and loving smiles. If I wanted to go somewhere, I could go and it would surely be an adventure.

Winter snows make time meaningless. I felt no urgency for spring because spring had disappeared into the invisible long-away future. The snows tucked me in deep and secure. The only time was now. As far as I was concerned the snows and the moment were an eternal companion.

Some might think that I should have been concerned about my financial condition. I was down to $65 by this time. Buying food had seriously dwindled my savings. But I wasn't concerned. What did I need money for? What I needed was food and warmth. I had those things. I was rich.

Chapter Nine

How to Pray for a Meal

I was rich, and I also was unusually hungry. My food was perfect, but it wasn't quite satisfying me. This was a big annoyance in my winter adventure—I couldn't quite put my finger on why I was always craving donuts. I could feel them calling me from their little refrigerator over the stream, which was near my cabin, which was near me. I was constantly overcome with their song and I would sneak out my door and stand there, ashamed, in the snow, cramming a stale, sugary, frozen donut in my mouth. Afterwards, their cries to be eaten would subside for a day or two.

One of the problems was getting a quick bite to eat. Most of my food took a couple hours of preparation. Necessity is the mother of invention. So my first invention was snack food—hoecakes and honey. Think of this recipe as protection against donuts.

I would make them by dumping a couple heaping spoonfuls of corn flour in a bowl and adding hot water until it was a pancake batter consistency (of course I didn't have eggs, they don't keep well in frozen wilderness cabins). The hotter the water the better, because it would soften the crunchy cornmeal. Then I'd pour spoonfuls of my primitive batter into a hot oiled pan and roll the pan around until the round bottom was evenly covered. Flip carefully with spatula. Smother with honey (butter if you have it) and chow down. Yum.

Unfortunately this was the only fast food I was able to invent. No matter how I went about it, rice, beans and lentils took a long time to cook for dinner. They also took a certain will power to chew and swallow day after day.

The nightly meal was a competition for Ray. He loved to have me over in his cabin when it was time to start cooking, which was usually earlier for him than it was for me. His food was instant. Portions were carefully calculated. Exactly what he needed was exactly what he would cook. First Ray would slice his canned meat into his small frying pan. He fried it carefully, patting the top with the spatula, and turning it, smiling gleefully at me until the juicy grease filled the pan. "Look, Coni," he would gloat. "Doesn't it look good?" Then he would slice a small baked potato and add the slices until they covered the bottom of the pan, one layer. Everything was patted regularly and turned until it was just right. Then he would eat, one small bite at a time, offering me a taste with each bite, which I would just as gleefully deny until supper was finished. Ray couldn't imagine such a thing as a vegetarian! Who had ever heard of such a thing! I would go home to my beans and hoecakes.

I boiled a lot of beans, fried cornbread, and occasionally baked some real bread. Ray's sausages and Spam never looked good to me, but my beans sure tasted awfully dry and plain. I smothered them with way too much cheese every time I could. Choking down my nightly dinner was a chore, and I was constantly hungry.

Slowly, I began to go nuts. I never felt full or satisfied, though I had plenty to eat. I was eating tons of starchy stuff and packing on weight. I tried fasting one day a week with no benefit. No amount of will power could hold me back from the cooler. I began carrying the donuts into my cabin, heating them slightly in the oven, sucking the cold jelly from the middle, then licking the powdered sugar off the sides—boy were they stale! I needed real food.

This was a self-induced survival situation, and I was discovering that a balanced diet is critical in a limited situation. I was in no danger, but I wasn't thriving. My food was too dry and blaaa. Beans, rice, corn: what could I really do with that stuff?

Fortunately, I had a lot of time and eventually learned to prepare a variety of foods from my few ingredients. After much experimentation (actually during my second winter on the creek) I happened across the perfect combination to satisfy my craving for "real food." The final solution was simple: traditional handmade corn tortillas, with fresh tofu and alfalfa sprouts (yum!). As I incorporated this combination into my diet my cravings subsided. It was whole fresh food from dried storage.

Further research has proven that I happened across a combination that fills all nutritional needs. It has a full array of protein, vitamins, and minerals—and a juicy bite. That juicy bite is so important. The flavorful bite of "real food" to the palate is critical in limited circumstances. That's why I call this the perfect survival food: it fills the needs of a long term, minimal diet.

Tofu was my first major food discovery. I learned how to make it by reading *The Book of Tofu*, by William Shurtleff. It's really simple. Soak some soybeans. After they are fully swelled grind them into a mush. I used to grind mine with an inexpensive hand grain-grinder that has metal plates. It's sort of like a meat grinder except it grinds the beans up much finer. (Now I do it in a blender with some of the boiling water.)

Dump the ground beans into boiling water (one quart water for one cup soaked beans), and stir continuously until it comes to a boil. Strain the milk out through a cloth and then add curdling salt (Epsom Salt or Nigari) to curd the milk. Then you strain the whey out of the curds, press it into shape and—voila—you have fresh tofu. It tastes a billion times better than the store-bought variety and storage is no problem because you can store dry soybeans anywhere that is mouse-proof.

The whey is a wonderful byproduct of making tofu. I read, in the *Book of Tofu*, that Japanese women use it to wash their faces and hair. I was always in search of natural-anything, and so jumped at the chance to try it. It works great. Just let the whey cool a bit and stick your head in the pot, or better yet, dump it all over your body. Rinse, fluff, and dry. You're done, and your hair is silky, clean, and fresh.

Another natural soap is Yucca root, which is indigenous to North America and was used by Indians (or so my books say). I once made natural soap from Yucca root, and it worked great, but it took too much effort. I'll go for soybean whey any day because it is simply a byproduct of making my daily food.

Recently, I've discovered another bonus from the wonderful soybean. It has been found that soybeans are a natural source of a compound that can be used as progesterone in the body. Progesterone is one of our female hormones that helps keep our other female hormone, estrogen, in check. Progesterone deficiencies make women feel grouchy, get white hair, grow facial hair, and get lumps in their breasts and uterus. Many ancient cultures, such as the Oriental ones with their soybeans, had diets rich in natural progesterone. This progesterone substance, which is called a diostogen, is readily absorbed through the skin. Another reason to wash with soybean whey!

In the east, the people who live close to the land and eat lots of vegetables and tofu, have significantly lower rates of cancer than the people of the technologically advanced West—particularly hormone-related cancers such as breast cancer and ovarian cancer. They also have less osteoporosis. We would all do well to follow their lead and make soy an integral part of daily life.

Many ancient cultures lived with only a minimum amount of foodstuffs, yet remained healthy and vital. Through trial and error the cultures managed to create balanced diets. Modern science is only beginning to see how vital this balance can be. During my second year in the cabin, I read of a study that was done on cornmeal. The study was begun because so many poor people who lived in the south were suffering from B vitamin deficiencies. The deficiencies were attributed to the fact that their diets consisted primarily of cornmeal. Corn is a grain that does not contain the full array of B vitamins.

Strangely enough, however, Native Americans of the southwest, who also ate a lot of corn, were not suffering from B vitamin deficiencies. The difference turned out to be that the natives would boil their corn with hardwood ash or lime before grinding it. A chemical reaction between the ash and the corn created B vitamins.

The article I read also contained a recipe, and so I learned how to make authentic corn tortillas.

Take a bunch of corn, soak it over night, and then boil it in water with a couple teaspoons of hardwood ash. Boil it until the hard outer skins start to fall off. Rinse the corn in cool water and use your hands to rub off the outer hulls. Rinse away the hulls then drain the corn. Grind corn in a grinder (same grinder used for tofu) and form into balls. Press flat in tortilla press and fry on top of a hot cookstove. Voila! Fresh corn tortillas.

The only thing missing from dinner now is a fresh, live vegetable. These are almost impossible to keep in a winter cabin because it freezes every night. It is a long way to the grocery store for fresh supplies. The solution is alfalfa sprouts, which are easy to make. Soak alfalfa seeds and rinse. Keep them in a dark spot and rinse them every day until they grow. Put them in the sun the last few days if you wish and the baby leaves will turn green.

It was a challenge to keep my sprouts from freezing and dying in the cold nights in the cabin. Wrapping the jar with a bunch of towels and keeping them in my bed, where my body provided a little warmth, did the trick, unless it got down to 40 below.

This is a dinner that takes quite a bit of preparation, but the result was a tasty, satisfying food. Once all the individual pieces were made I had instant food to assemble. Here's how I put it together:

Heat a tablespoon of oil in a frying pan on medium high heat. Quickly toss the corn tortillas, one at a time, in the hot oil to soften. Set aside and keep warm by covering with a towel. Add some more oil and sauté onions lightly (if you've got them). Slice tofu into long strips and fry until golden brown on both sides. Sprinkle generously with soy sauce and paprika. Wrap in hot tortilla. Top with fresh alfalfa sprouts. A little vinegar and oil dressing makes this a totally yummy meal. Too bad I could never get Ray to take a bite. But I would pat my tofu pieces, as I turned them over, gloating at him for dinner.

Prayer

This brings me to a story about prayer. This happened many years later, when I had small children, and lived in the wilderness of central Idaho. I grew huge gardens in the summer and canned food. Almost everything we ate was made entirely from scratch—pure homegrown food. It would take me all day just to grind the wheat, make bread, tend the garden, and prepare supper. All my life energy went into preparing food for my family.

One day we went to town, Salmon, Idaho, and they were having a parade. People were selling things out on the sidewalks and the kids wanted hotdogs from the hotdog stand. I bought hotdogs to go around. Everybody grabbed one and I grabbed mine. I cradled my hotdog in my hand and, totally out of habit, not thinking about it at all, gave the hotdog a look.

It was the same look that I always gave the food I had prepared from scratch, though I never realized I was doing it. It wasn't verbal, there were no conscious words involved, but it was a little acknowledgment of knowing where the food had come from. Knowing the soil it had grown in, the water and sun that had fed it, the hands that had picked and prepared it. I was looking at the hotdog with the same feeling I looked at my own prepared food. I was so used to feeling praise for my food that I showered the hotdog with the same feeling. Then I noticed that in my hand was a hotdog. I had no idea where the pieces for this hotdog may have come from. I almost withdrew the praise, then changed my mind. I smiled at the doggie and bun and took a big bite. Yumm. That day I understood the meaning of prayer; it took ten years of preparing my own food for me to get it, but I got it that day. Prayer is acknowledging the universality of a thing, where it came from. If you want to call that god, then thank god for your food. That is prayer.

Bread Stories

During my first year in the cabin, bread was a food for special occasions. It took so much time to make it, and then I would have a whole loaf that I had to eat by myself. It would be pretty dry by the time I was done. In my later years, feeding a family, it became an every-day event to make bread. Today I live in the lowlands, at an elevation of four thousand feet (low to me at least). Up on Homestake Creek, at 9000 feet, the altitude made bread baking a challenge. I learned to love nice hard, substantial loaves while living there.

Throughout my life I have had a continual bonding with bread. It seems to be more than just food. It's a presence. Maybe that's because it is alive. It grows. The yeast in bread needs nourishment, it reproduces. It works hard and pushes the bread up. I swear it has whims. Sometimes it behaves in one way, sometimes another. Just like I do. Maybe that's why I think of bread in the same way I think of myself, as a collection of stories.

I remember one of my first bonding episodes with bread. I must have been in the fourth grade. I went to a Catholic school without a cafeteria so we all brought our lunches to school. My friends all had white bread because they came from normal families. My mom was different; she was a health food nut and my sandwiches were made with whole wheat bread.

Then I read the book Heidi. In many ways Heidi is a bread story. One of the main subplots revolves around the Grandmother's wish for the kind of bread that rich people eat, good white bread. The poor people in Heidi ate hard, dark bread that was tough on the Grandmother's teeth. I felt very dramatic and tragic because I had dark bread for my sandwiches, so I must have been just like Heidi. My little kid mind decided that whole-wheat bread was proof that we were poor. Hanging my head in important shame

I related this fact to my friends at school who were suitably impressed and offered me the appropriate sympathy.

I managed to squeeze a week or two of sympathy from my friends until the day I mentioned my plight to my mother. She informed me that whole wheat bread was much more expensive than white bread. In fact, not only was it more expensive, it was very difficult to buy at that time and she had to drive halfway across town just to find a suitably healthy whole wheat bread for the family. I marched right back to school and gloated this fact over my friends. Obviously, we were considerably richer than they were because I ate expensive whole wheat bread. They only had white; they hung their heads in shame. I offered no sympathy and ate my bread with glee.

I remember an earlier bonding with bread, perhaps in the first grade. I went to a friend's house. As the door opened to let me in, I was engulfed by a fragrance that captured my nostrils and made me completely awake. Her mother had actually *baked* bread and just taken it out of the oven. She sliced it into thick chunks, slathered it with butter and honey, and let me have some! To this day I remember the thrill of my first whiff of home-baked bread. Every time I slice into a hot and crispy loaf I feel that same childish peace and security. I always have the first crusty piece hot with butter and honey. That's what it is about bread. Baking bread makes the world seem a friendly place, a nourishing haven.

I had already baked bread for years before I moved into my cabin. As a beginner, I made a big deal about it. I read recipes, actually measured the ingredients, got my water to the exact right temperature, timed my kneading to a full five minutes, rose it exactly twice in scientifically controlled heat, studied different ways to fold my final loaf to prevent bubble holes, sprinkled stuff on top, and thunked it like a pumpkin to make sure it was baked right. My exact bread-making skills sometimes worked and sometimes didn't. I couldn't figure out why. Every bread failure caused me to tighten my philosophy of bread making. I was determined to MAKE it work.

My life has been a series of fanatic bread-making theories. At one time I ground all my wheat with a hand grinder. I eventually graduated to a motor-driven grinder and made such healthy bread you could build a house with it. We had fiber all right! I remember once deciding that the bread must be picking up my psychic moods and that it wouldn't rise if I was "negative." I tortured myself, trying to be happy as I pounded the dough into submission.

Several years ago I got a job in a restaurant. This restaurant was famous all over town for its wonderful bread. The making of this bread was supposed to be a secret, but I watched closely and over time my amazement grew. You have never seen such tortured bread dough in all your life! This bread was hated, neglected, forgotten, and slopped around with drunken carelessness. The loaves were white and made from commercial, frozen dough. This dough was physically abused every day, but it was wonderful and tasty. Enthusiastic customers proclaimed it "The Best Bread EVER!" The only trick with that bread was that it was baked in a very hot, 600-degree oven.

I was forced to face facts and drop my long-nourished bread ego. The truth is, bread dough could care less. In fact, the more you torture and neglect it, the happier it is. I started neglecting my bread at home and it responded with glee. Taking a clue from my restaurant experience, I gave up on my stuck idea of what bread should be and surrendered to my pathetic sticky dough. I have made perfect bread ever since.

The first trick is to rise the bread slowly in a place that is not too warm. I remember once, I must have killed the yeast because my loaf didn't rise. I let it sit around and sit around, and didn't worry about it. After about two days it suddenly rose—I guess there must have been two good yeasts left in there and they finally got the urge to reproduce. I baked it and it was just fine. One other time, I completely forgot I was making bread. As we were getting ready for bed my daughter, Kacey, looked up and noticed a long, brown ooze dripping down over the shelf out of the pan where I had left it to rise. Oops. Well, I sure wasn't about to stay up and bake the stuff. I crammed it back into a bowl and stuck it in the refrigerator. I tried it again the next day and it was just fine—a bit sour but, hey, in some places you pay extra for that.

My brother Bill has a theory that every civilization in human history is the result of a good recipe. This is because some recipe would happen to have all the nutrients and comfort levels needed to sustain the human body in a healthy state. Bread was the invention of Europe. Tofu was the invention of the East. Corn tortillas were the invention of South American Indians. Thanks to all people.

Chapter Ten

How to Howl at the Moon

Winter was getting on a bit now. I was in my little cabin, I had food, I had donuts, I had snow, and I still had $65. I had given up all ideas of worrying about money. I was set. As far as I was concerned, my career choice was working out so perfectly that the word "career" never entered my mind.

I am writing this book now in a distant time and place from my winters at Homestake Creek. Those of you reading this book who have a more practical approach to life than me can make a pretty good guess that earning money and making a living has been quite a problem for me since I've come out of the snow. My initial self-training out of high school was in poverty, and I trained myself quite well. Yes, it's true. I've earned less money in the last 20 years than many of you earn in one year. Running around naked in a meadow does not put you in the same tax bracket as an astrophysicist. This has created some major challenges for me.

Lately, I've had some major breakthroughs about my attitudes towards the almighty dollar. Deep down inside, my overriding attitude about money is that I am rich. Small things make me rich and I see them. In my deep subconscious money has so little importance that I barely give it emotional concern. The existence of money to me is less important than a fly buzzing around my head on a warm summer's day. It's not even the fly; it's the air that the fly buzzes in. This is an attitude that only one who thinks she is rich can have.

While living on Homestake Creek I never thought of what I didn't have. I was only focused on what I did have.

Light the Lamp

Days are short and nights are long in the winter. For light I had two things, a kerosene lantern and a supply of candles. This was a big step up from my tipi days.

In the lanterns, that year, we were burning fuel oil instead of kerosene. This was Ray's idea. He bought our supply of fuel oil in big, refillable cans. The fuel oil was cheaper, and through many years of experimentation he had decided that the fuel oil burned with a brighter light. I didn't know one way or the other. I had used kerosene lamps before, and remembered them to be brighter than the reddish glow that came from my fuel oil lamp, but who was I to say anything? I half suspect that Ray's choice had more to do with his growing cataracts than with actual wattage from the lamps. Maybe the red glow from the fuel oil looked brighter from his lenses. Nevertheless, I honored his fuel oil choice and enjoyed my lantern.

Ray was a man to be listened to because he had spent years watching. One of his occupations, through the years of living on Homestake Creek, was timing the rising of the moon. He informed me, on a fairly regular basis, that the moon would rise exactly 43 minutes later each night as it worked through its cycle.

I had no reason to doubt that. Ray had an absolutely perfect pocket watch that he had received when he retired from the railroad. He'd spent years timing the moon, which was as good a job as any for his retirement watch out on Homestake Creek.

"See Coni," he'd say. We were leaning on our brooms after shoveling the path, watching as the moon rose over the eastern mountains. "Forty three minutes." He would tap his watch knowingly and give me a nod and a smile. Slowly the watch would go back in the pocket, a gift of great pride, and we would go back to sweeping the trails.

Ray's choice on the fuel oil, Ray's count of the moon. He was the master. I was the explorer.

I ended up using candles at night for reading more often than I used my fuel oil lamp. It was hard to keep the wick clean in the lamp and I often got as much black smoke as light out of it. Candles gave a whiter, brighter light that better lit the page of a book.

My book supply was an assortment of things that friends in town had lent me. I made a few trips into town that winter simply for an exchange of books. One friend lent me a whole collection, a series of eight books, about a monk from Tibet who could do astral traveling. This monk ended up taking over a body of some guy in England to finish his work in enlightening the world or something like that. The books fascinated me and drew me into a whole new world of Tibetan mysticism, and yet something seemed a little odd about them. I couldn't quite buy the whole storyline.

I had another book that explained meditation techniques, so I decided to explore that part of reality by myself instead of relying on the opinions of mythical Tibetan monks. One of the exercises was a meditation where you cover your right nostril with your thumb, breath in through the left, then cover the left nostril with the big finger, and breathe out through the right. I don't remember the actual technique now. What I do remember was the warning given with this meditation; that it only be done by adepts under the guidance of a master meditator.

As you can well imagine, there were no master meditators within a thousand miles of my little snowed-in cabin. You can also imagine how much fear I gave to the warning. Humph. I was going to try it any way. There I sat, on my little bunk bed, poking one nostril after the other closed with my fingers: watching and waiting for something terrible to happen.

Looking back at these meditation attempts I have to laugh at my good fortune. In every case it might not be true, but in my case the lack of spiritual guidance was the thing that plunged me into more and more awareness. A guide would have made it too easy, would have given me some sort of a goal to be striving for. As it was, my meditation was both a challenge to whatever 'terrible thing' it was that would come and get me if I dared to perform this forbidden technique, and an extreme watchfulness to see this 'terrible thing' before it came, so I could duck.

The watchfulness *was* the answer. Expanded awareness comes from watchfulness. I was tricking myself into awakening. From that winter on, I have never been able to be fooled by anybody's interpretation of spirituality. That clearness of vision has saved me from lots of foolishness.

This same spiritual daring has been with me since childhood. I can remember, as a small child in Catholic schools, challenging the nuns. I have always been drawn to religiousness, fascinated by the saints, intrigued by the nuns. One day my teacher said we couldn't experience God because he is infinite and our minds could never grasp the infinite. Don't even bother.

"Oh yeah?" I thought. I took it as a challenge. I had plenty of extra time sitting in mass every morning before school, so I started imagining bigger and bigger: off through space—looking for God. I was going to prove that I *could* imagine the infinite! I traveled with my thoughts out and out with my imagination. Further and further into the infinite. Larger and larger: through the universe: convinced that if I just kept going I could reach infinity and prove the nuns wrong!

Imagining infinity is a challenging task for a 10-year-old, but I had plenty of time in morning mass. I would imagine myself out and out and out, then 'Pop!' I would lose concentration and be right back in my regular head. Rats. Each time I lost concentration I was right back where I started—with myself. I tried unsuccessfully for days. I realized that something else needed to be done—so I cheated. I started expanding, after each break in concentration, from where I had broken off—from way out in space to bigger and bigger. It was a smooth trick, and working quite well, but infinity was still far away. Day after day passed and I'd hardly moved. Something else was needed.

Then the answer came. I realized that if I could start where I had left off—why not go ahead and start at the end. Why not start right *in* infinity. Pop! There I was. The final solution took less than a millisecond. Perhaps it was true that the mind could not experience infinity—but with a simple trick *I* certainly could!

See, I *would* have made a good astrophysicist.

After that, I must have been even more annoying to the poor nuns who were trying to educate me. I've never been very good at keeping my mouth shut when something doesn't make sense to me. I remember another Catholic school event. Sister Irmena was trying to teach us about God.

Imagine all the rows of good Catholic children at our desks. We are dressed identically: girls in blue plaid pleated wool skirts with bibs. Our shirts are white and our sweaters blue with a patch on the left breast. The boys are in black pants with a crease ironed up the front of the legs. Their shirts are white and sweaters blue with a patch. We are well behaved. We stand up whenever the priest enters the room and say in unison, "Good morning, Father."

We are also some of the best and the brightest that the suburbs have to offer; we often talk amongst ourselves concerning world-shattering matters such as, "Do nuns have hair?"

I'm at my desk and Sister Irmena is teaching about God. Sister Irmena is a white face sunk in a long habit of black. She has round wire rimmed glasses that flash with the light when she turns towards the windows. Her pointed black boots click under the sweeping black of her skirt as she paces past the desks of timid children. Her name has the word "mean" in it. So did her thin, tight lips.

Sister Irmena is telling us, again, that God is infinite. We can only have faith that God exists because we can't actually find him.

"Why not?" I ask, and she is aghast.

"Because you can't. People try but no one can do it."
"Why not?" I ask again. "If God loves us he will let us find him."
"You CAN'T."
"Why not?"
"YOU can't"
"Why not?"

Finally Sister Irmena loses her cool. She glides down the aisle in a smooth black motion, and shoves her white nun face directly in front of my 10-year-old bangs. "You can never look upon the face of God," she hisses, "Because if you do, the sight is so horrible that you can *never* look away."

The world stands still. There is the nun's face and my face. I remain silent.

Inside I think, *"Cool. This I gotta see."* She had admitted to me that you *can* find God. Someone must have done it to report back what it was like.

I could do it too.

I had the same attitude about my meditations. This I could do. The more dangerous the better. God should beware when he challenges me!

Later, I would find that Sister Irmena was quite right in her assessment. 'Horrible' is a much better adjective to use for God than 'beautiful.' If a person is looking for a beautiful god then they will miss that half of the world that doesn't meet qualifications of beautiful. When things are going wrong we will wonder, "Where has God gone?"

But more important than that, beautiful doesn't have the same attraction and pull that horrible has. When something is beautiful you have the choice of whether you look at it or not. It can compare against other beautiful things. You can look and say, "That is beautiful. That is lovely, but maybe if it had a bit more red over here." Yawn.

Horrible is just plain horrible. You've gotta look. Like when you have to look at a traffic accident when you pass. You have to look at the television when people start screaming. The attraction is too strong. It pulls you in, it draws you, and it magnetizes you. God has this same magnetism. Once you see God, the oneness that is everywhere, in all things, and around all things, you can never look away. You can never look away for the simple reason that there is nowhere to look that isn't God, the magnetism is total. You can never look away.

My meditations gave me a better skill in looking.

Howling Coyotes

Another book I had in my cabin was Dracula. Some friend had recently read it and told me that I had to read it too. When pinching my nostrils got boring, I snuggled up with my candle and Dracula.

I'm the kind of person who can sit down and read a whole book in a day. I started Dracula around noon and kept going on and on through flickering candles in the night.

Dusk was coming on when I reached the part where Dracula comes in through the girl's window. Simply leaving a window unlatched is an invitation for Dracula to come in! I took a break from my reading to make sure my one window was shut and latched. Then I double-checked it.

The one window in my cabin was to the right of the door, between the door and the bunkbed where I sat reading. Under the window was my wooden crate with its flickering candle.

The candle has burnt a quarter of the way down, used wax curling from the sides and dripping onto the crate. Shadows flick on the log walls and cast darkness into the bits of old rag sticking out from under the caulking wood wedges. I get up and add a few more sticks to the fire. A little puff of smoke is let into the cabin when I raise the round lid off the stovetop to insert the long-burning pine.

Levi and Sheila see me move. They raise their heads from their paws and flick their ears. I'm back to reading.

Dracula bites the girl's neck and things go badly for her. Everyone is being chased and bitten. The characters meet one impossible situation after the other. Dracula is so creepy because he seems nice enough and everyone is fooled. They don't even know they are in danger! The hair rises on the back of my neck. Terrible things happen in the dark castle, and then we are all running through the dark shadowy woods. Dracula is chasing us to suck out our souls. The forest is nothing but blackness, trees reaching out to grab us as we run, and off in the distance, suddenly the wolf pack starts howling.

At that exact moment, the coyotes of Homestake Creek start howling at the moon. The words of Dracula are pouring into my red rimmed eyes by the flickering candle, and coyote howls in my ears. Whoa!!!

I sat up and slammed the book shut. Creepy! Levi and Sheila are sitting up taunt. They see my jolt and start howling with their wild cousins. Levi has a high yip, Sheila a low tuneless yowl. There are howls in my head, howls outside the cabin, howls inside the cabin. Gulp—I check the window latch again. Time to come back to reality. I blink my tired eyes, laugh at the coyotes and shush the dogs. Levi and Sheila rest.

I have to finish the book that night because there is no way I'm ever going to sleep again. The coyotes have fits of yapping through the night. The candle burned until it was a tiny, flickering stub. I'm very late to sweep the trails the next morning!

Chapter Eleven

How to Move an Outhouse

One day, at the beginning of that first winter, Ray presented me with a gift.

The beginning of winter wasn't when the first snows fell, but that moment when we were not able to drive out any more. There was no question about that moment. A huge snowfall came in the night and reduced our travel options from car to foot. We didn't sweep the trails that morning, but got out shovels. Neither Ray nor I mentioned the obvious. We just looked at the deep snow and nodded our heads knowingly. Ray lightly clicked his tongue. I think we were both a little bit relieved. The fast world had come to stillness.

Ray shoveled off in one direction, and I worked, shovel-full by shovel-full, in mine. I put my shovel away and was heading back to my cabin when I noticed Ray marching down the trail in my direction. We met near the stream.

"Coni," Ray said, handing me a thick stick about three feet long. "Put this in your outhouse." He gave me a knowing smile and no explanation. As he turned back to his cabin he exuded a delightful pride. Obviously he had just shared a tremendous secret with me.

I had no idea what the stick was for. Ray's confidence told me that when the moment came I would know what to do with my stick. I took it over to my outhouse and leaned it up against an inside corner.

Done. Some sort of vital mission had been accomplished. As winter moved on my stick sat in its corner, keeping its secret to itself. The days got colder and colder.

The outhouse situation on the mining claim was pretty straightforward. There were two outhouses. One was over by Ray's cabin and it was for him. The other outhouse was toward the driveway from my cabin. It was between my little cabin and the big cabin. To get to it, I walked down into a small draw. This outhouse was for me and for any guests.

I've used many outhouses in my life and this one on Homestake Creek was the cleanest I'd ever seen. It was a little wooden house, a one-seater, with little smell. The hole was hardly full. I assumed this was the result of light use.

While living in the tipi I had used the method of disposal that Bev and Joe had taught me. Head off into the woods in a different direction each day, dig a little hole, make your deposit, fill and leave the place as unnoticeable as possible. Joe informed me that this was the way the Indians did it. They never dug one hole for everybody's poop the way the white man does.

It seemed to me that this method would quickly create a mysterious, hidden circle of poo around any Indian tipi settlement. Maybe it was the thing that kept the tribes constantly moving to new home sites. It does have certain ecological and fertilization plusses for people who live with lots of wide-open spaces.

Learning the Obvious

As a child, I was not born with an inborn wisdom of how to shit in the woods. We were quite an outdoorsy family, but still, I was raised with the flush toilet. At our cabin in Wyoming, where we would spend a few weeks each summer, we had a very primitive, but still workable sit-down outhouse. As a small child, I naturally assumed that people had to sit on something in order to go to the bathroom.

I remember going on camping trips and facing the dilemma of exactly what I was supposed to do out in the woods. My siblings and I came up with the solution of sitting on a fallen log. Picture us, if you will, hanging our little rears off a fallen log and completing our morning necessities without falling.

I had a more difficult problem than my brothers. They knew how to stand up to pee. I was always looking for a fallen tree.

As embarrassing as it is, I learned the proper technique from a book. Duh! It's so obvious! Real people squat. It's as simple as that.

The correct way to piss in the woods is as follows: For boys it's obvious—just write your name wherever you are. For girls, squat, positioning yourself so you are facing downhill because there is going to be a little river that you want to run *away* from your feet. Afterwards, you can wipe yourself carefully with a handy twig, leaf, or smooth rock. Do not wipe yourself with poison ivy.

Let me repeat that. If you think you may ever be in a situation to pee in the woods, make sure you know how to recognize poison ivy and poison oak. It presents itself as a very attractive wiping tool. It has sets of three leaves and in the fall turns itself into gorgeous reds, yellow, and oranges.

If you use toilet paper you should bury the paper in a little hole that you dig with a stick, or under a large rock. Don't leave it lying around, please. Use a natural paper and it will disintegrate into the woods quickly enough. It's easy.

Urine, itself, is not an extremely toxic substance. You can pee fairly close to a river or stream, but preferably not *into* the river or stream. If lots of people use an area it is best to take a nice long hike before doing your business. One person's pee will disappear fairly quickly into the environment. Twenty people, day after day, will stink up the place.

For pooping, get a good healthy distance from any water supply, because this stuff is not benign! Find a stick and dig a hole big enough to accommodate your pile and any toilet paper you will use. Squat over your hole and make your donation. Cover the hole back up with the dirt that you removed. If possible cover with a rock so no one will step in it.

People in pre-industrial cultures squat to poop. In the East, bathrooms are often holes in the ground that you squat over. This is the natural position for the human body in relieving itself. Using this position can cure a person of constipation and hemorrhoids that are caused by straining in an unnatural position.

I once read that women who squat to poop have an easier time having babies because their organs are better positioned for the job; their legs and pushing mechanisms are more flexible. I think this is true. I made a point of squatting to poop whenever I was pregnant, and had almost effortless childbirth experiences.

Squatting in the woods has more advantages than simple health benefits. You can see things from this position. Once, two years later, in the spring, when I was in Northern Idaho, where the forests grow faster with more rain and a low altitude, I saw a pine tree sprout. I saw it only because of squatting to pee. I had gone a bit away from other people and taken my squatting position under an ancient Yellow Pine. As I peed I gazed at the forest floor around me. There, six inches away from my foot was a fallen pinecone. Out of it, curving down and then up, came a juicy sprout. It looked just like a mung bean sprout. I reached out and touched the little leaves, careful not to crush or harm this wonder. Wait till I tell my friends!

A pine tree sprout! I had seen a pine tree sprout—a miracle of nature. Under a tree that was hundreds of years old I saw its brand new, natural baby, probably two days old. No matter how much I tried, nobody else seemed to share my enthusiasm.

Nose Blowing

There are other forms of elimination that need to be relearned when living out in the woods. The forest is not a natural place for tissue or tissue-like plants. How do you suppose the Indians blew their noses?

I tried to figure this one out on my own while I was still living in Leadville. I was in training, preparing myself for my upcoming move into the woods. This was after Bev and Joe had given me my tipi, and I was determined to make my break from civilization in the spring. It was a cold winter day, and I was off from work and walking up the hill towards my house. The cold air made my nose run.

I was covered with coats, mittens, scarves, and hats. I didn't have a tissue or handkerchief with me. Sniffing didn't do any good—the nose-run was too big. What to do? I started to wonder about natural Indians. How did they blow their noses? The only nose blowing I had ever seen in my life was into a tissue or handkerchief. I worked my well-educated mind to the max and couldn't come up with a solution. The best idea I had was pulling leaves off a bush and blowing my nose into them. Yo! Not a workable solution! Especially since the only leaves available in the middle of the winter are pine needles! Snot spurted everywhere, all over my glasses, all over my hands. I *really* hurried the rest of the way home!

I couldn't come up with the answer to this problem out of my own mind. Not enough data. No book, no encyclopedia, holds the answer. I didn't know any natural people. I had to give up.

Ray Kelly, without ever knowing I was looking for an answer, gave it to me one day. He needed to clear his nose, so he simply leaned over, placed a finger firmly on one nostril, and give a big blow. A quick change of fingers onto the other nostril cleaned the other passage. If done with skill this technique leaves hardly a drip. A quick wipe, with a handkerchief or sleeve, cleans any residue. Clean, quick, simple. I couldn't figure it out until I saw it. Imagine that. So many mysteries have simple solutions.

How to Move an Outhouse

I've known many outhouses in my time. Some people like to decorate them up with candles and wise sayings. I'm of the opinion that outhouses should be left alone except for the occasional cleaning. Anything that is put out there will become irrevocably stinky and should never be touched again. The only things that should be in an outhouse are toilet paper and a stick, even in a clean smelling outhouse like the one I had on Homestake Creek.

That outhouse was strangely clean, all by itself.

Later on, when spring came to Homestake Creek I discovered the secret. As the snow started melting a quick and persistent stream of water formed along the gullies and ran straight down, into the outhouse hole, and out to the meadow below. The grass grew exceptionally green and lush down there. Every spring that outhouse got a flush. Not proper outhouse etiquette for ground water considerations. What to do? This outhouse had been there for decades, I sure couldn't move it!

I did move an outhouse once. In later years, I lived on a remote homestead in the Mountains of Idaho. The Beaver Creek buildings were not arranged in the best way and the outhouse was too close to one of the cabins. Our friends Nan and Courtney were staying in the cabin and complaining of the smell.

This outhouse did not have a yearly spring cleaning (thankfully!) and had filled up with solid waste. We discussed digging a new hole several times, but the prospect of chopping through the tough rocky mountain soil stopped us from beginning the project.

Then, one day I detected a change in the air, which eventually became distinguishable as an engine slowly traveling up the road. Finally, a backhoe appeared at the top of the hill. Opportunity was knocking! I ran out and waved down the driver. He was taking the machine up the creek to work on a mine up there. Negotiations began. What could I give him for digging me a hole? It was a friendly game since, out in the woods, neighborliness is the only coin paid for favors.

He was there with a backhoe. I needed a hole. There was no question that the favor needed to be done. Still, something had to be exchanged.

It was cherry picking time, so I offered to pay him with two fresh cherry pies. He accepted and turned the backhoe into the yard. It took less than ten minutes to dig a perfect outhouse-size hole. Then quickly my benefactor was off on his way. We were both convinced that we had gotten the best part of the deal. I had a hole that would have been impossible for me to dig, he had two fresh cherry pies (an impossible to find treat out in the wilderness) delivered to his remote mining claim the next day.

Now that we had a hole, how in the world could we move the old outhouse building over there? Living on the site at the time were Nan, Courtney, John, and I. A few days later our friends Brad and Clark stopped by. Six people were enough to declare an outhouse moving party!

This particular outhouse was a work of art. It was a log outhouse. The overlapping ends of the logs were cut into an attractive curve at the bottom. The building was small, but all that solid wood was going to be heavy.

Our plan was to have one man on each corner. Nan and I were in the middle of the long sides, front and back. We positioned ourselves and gave a big call of, "One, two, three!" Up came the outhouse, revealing the foul hole underneath.

Nobody was in the mood to move slowly. We started our march across the yard, in a direct beeline to the new position. Two steps into the trip we heard a loud bleat from Brad. The outhouse suddenly became heavier and tilted towards the back. Looking back, there was Brad saving himself from a fate worse than death! We had almost dragged him into the hole!

Remember: if you ever try to move an outhouse you have to plan your getaway from the original hole! You must go straight away—a kitty-corner journey is going to ruin one person!

Recovering from our mishap, we carried the little building over to the new hole and set it up. I thought I was in for a delightful treat with this new, clean position. But it smelled as bad as it always had—even before the new hole was used. The wood held the stink.

I never needed a stick in that outhouse. Five thousand feet lower in altitude made all the difference.

Once, in this outhouse, I saw a grasshopper shit. That may not seem like such a marvelous thing, but tell me, have you ever seen a grasshopper in the process of relieving itself? A wild grasshopper?

It was late summer, in one of those years when the grasshoppers were big. I was sitting on my hole (this particular outhouse was a two-seater) and a grasshopper jumped up on the seat, over by the other hole. It was a big grasshopper. It looked at me and scowled. I was quite involved on my own hole and didn't want to move to shoo it off, so I scowled back. The grasshopper blinked and appeared to relax slightly. Then it started to wiggle its behind. This caught my attention as it was wiggling its rear just the way a yellow jacket does. Then its bottom split open slightly, like two leaves parting, and a little brown spike slowly started protruding. Quickly I ran my encyclopedia of stored information through my mind. This was a grasshopper? Right? Grasshoppers don't sting do they? Am I sure this is a grasshopper? That sure looked like a stinger emerging from its rear. I sat there, vulnerable, while the spike grew longer. Then, all of the sudden, it fell off.

The grasshopper looked at me again. Its eyes slanted slightly, the way a cat's will when getting out of the cat-box. Then it hopped off, back to its grasshopper world. I was transfixed. Grasshopper poop! I had seen a grasshopper poop! The long thin turd remained next to me on the bench seat.

I finished my business and rushed into the house, searching for a suitable container. Baby food jar! Yes! I grabbed the jar and rushed back to the outhouse, scooped up my prize and sealed the lid. I was rich! This was a thing that nobody else ever had. I proudly stored it on a shelf in my house.

Visitors were promptly informed of its importance. No one seemed to get it.

Years later, when my son started school, we were very poor and he was hard pressed for something for Show-And-Tell. He took the jar with its treasure, not quite sure if this was going to be a hit. Some other kid grabbed the jar from him and shook out the contents. I lost my prize. But I really had a treasure at one time.

Once, I had a friend who bought a piece of land. His goal was to build an entire house from bits and pieces of things he found. This was the late 80s during the barn wood fad. He built his house and invited us over for a viewing.

Proudly he drove us down an impassable road in his four-wheel-drive truck. The house was small, but nice and tidy. He ushered us inside—and the stink hit me fast. What in the world? Ted proudly bragged about the old barnwood that lined the kitchen. The woodwork was impeccable. Neatly mitered corners and flush edges of slab wood were on the wall. He had found an old outhouse for his free barn wood. Phew! He was a smoker and couldn't smell a thing. I told him to quickly remodel his house—yeeze!

Trust me. Outhouses do not qualify as old barnwood!

But back to Homestake Creek. I had a clean, sweet-smelling outhouse with a stick leaning against the wall in the corner, and it kept getting colder.

Coldness has a mind of its own. It makes things solid and brittle. In the deep, deep cold magic things happen. Ice crystals grow up from the snow like a tiny glittering forest. Cold and wet can get inside a tree limb and cut it like a knife with expansion. Sit quietly in a cold forest for long enough and you may hear a crack, like the shot of a gun as a limb bursts from a tree.

Down inside the bowels of my outhouse the cold was playing its game. Each deposit I made would go straight down and land on the previous day's deposit. Day after day this creation grew upward towards the hole which supported my sitting. It grew straight and tall, with alarming rapidity. About a month into my winter journey I knew what I must do with my stick. The stack had grown to within an inch of my sitting hole. All it took was one enthusiastic whack from my stick and I could again sit on the seat of my outhouse.

Problem solved.

Party Time

Late in December, I made my goodbyes to Ray. I was heading into Leadville to see some people and attend a few Christmas parties. I told him I would be gone several days. I wasn't too happy with my food supplies and was thinking of going all the way into Denver for another trip to the health food store. At the very least I would make some serious purchases at the grocery store in Leadville to ease my gnawing hunger.

I packed my 65 dollars into my backpack, strapped on my skis and headed off into the cold.

Chapter Twelve

How to Find Financial Insecurity

I hitched into town and discovered that there was a party that night at the house on Sixth Street. I stuck my backpack in a corner near the door and joined my friends. We had a lot to talk about. Everyone came over.

I was in the kitchen at midnight, when in through the back door walked the three tallest guys I'd ever seen. It was John, Courtney, and Tim. Courtney was 6'5", Tim 6'4", and John 6'3". They were skinny and long, with beards sticking out from under their stocking caps. John and I hit it off and ended up talking all night. He had lived in a tipi a few summers ago. Now he was working at the mine. Early in the morning we took a long walk to watch the sun come up, then went over to his house and ate leftover soup for breakfast. He lived two blocks from the house on Sixth Street with his brother Jay and Jay's wife, Kathy. Kathy was seven months pregnant.

After soup, I began to feel my tiredness, so I went back to Sixth Street to find a place to lay my sleeping bag down and get some sleep. My 65 dollars was gone from my pack!

Shock! Someone from the party had ripped me off. More painful than the fact that I was suddenly broke was the idea that one of my friends, whom I believed all loved me, must have done it. Every cent was gone; I had never thought to put any money in my pockets. I was absolutely broke, and cast into limbo. What to do? There was going to be no trip for groceries; my plans came to a screeching halt.

I told everyone what had happened, cried, and slept in my sleeping bag until afternoon. When I woke up I still couldn't think of what to do except go back to Homestake Creek and adjust. I was out of cheese and fresh food, but had plenty of dry stuff left, so I wouldn't starve. My instinct was to crawl into a hole and lick my wounds. I needed time to think.

Then Janet came over. She'd been at the party the night before, but I hardly knew her. When she heard what had happened she decided that she needed to help. She invited me up to a poker party at her house that night.

The last thing in the world I wanted was another party, but she insisted. I didn't want to go. I had no money to play with, didn't know how to play, and didn't consider poker as a way to earn a living. But Janet insisted and insisted and insisted. She was one of those types of gals who make up their minds about what other people should do and there is no arguing against her. Finally, I gave in. Besides, I was feeling depressed, and the effort of hitchhiking to Homestake Creek and walking into my cabin seemed too much for this day.

I'm not sure if this is true for other people's lives, but I know that in mine there are defining moments, moments that set the tone for the future, moments that pull me into a repeating pattern of behavior.

I caved to my better judgment and went to this party. In fact, Janet came and picked me up in her car to make sure I would be there. She fed me dinner to make sure I stayed. I sat on the couch feeling uncomfortable and out-of-place and watched a group of guys I hardly knew start to play poker. They invited me into the game but I didn't want to play. I didn't have any money to bet with. My mind was not in a winning mode. There was something broken inside.

As soon as the poker party was in full swing (timed perfectly so no one could leave) Janet went over to the table and made her announcement. I was an unfortunate victim who had been robbed. She thought it was the job of the poker party to save me and started insisting to them that however much money was won in the poker game that night would go to me.

"No." I didn't want it. I wasn't sure how to get my bearings about my money, but this didn't sound right. Janet was full of the righteousness of giving. She knew I didn't have a penny to my name and that lent her power. She also had surprise on her side. I resisted.

Janet insisted.

I resisted. The boys in the poker party were embarrassed and scowling.

Janet's willpower was in full swing. Mine was weakened by too much surprise.

I don't remember who was at the poker party that night, but I remember the feel of the looks of their faces. They were trapped—nobody could be a jerk and refuse this impoverished cause that was right in front of them; nobody was happy about it either. I read the defiance in their faces.

One guy voiced his displeasure, "If she wants the money from poker—she ought to win it." I knew I was incapable of winning it. I couldn't leave. We were all trapped. The boys reluctantly agreed to the plan.

It must have been the worst game of poker ever played. The players got no joy from a winning hand. I couldn't bear to watch from the couch where I sat in silence. All I wanted was to go back to sleep. At the end of the game I was handed the pile of money from the center of the table. Clenched in my fist was just over thirty-three dollars, mostly in change. It was the first time in my life I can remember my hands not having any weight. I put the money in my pocket and left as quickly as I could. I walked down the cold hill, in the dark, to the Sixth Street house.

The money sat like a lump in my pocket. Now I was numb from my loss, guilty, and greedy for the money at the same time. It would have been better for me to hike penniless back to Homestake Creek and recoup. No telling what sort of financial decisions I would have arrived at, but at least I would have had my dignity. As it was I was able to stop at the grocery store the next day and spend the ill-gotten money on supplies, then limp my way home.

Job Time

I regained my composure after a couple of weeks blanketed in the snow at Homestake Creek. My future was obvious. I needed to go into town, get a job and make myself some money—but not too much. I was now viewing this as a temporary setback.

I made my goodbyes to Ray, hiked into town and put my homelessness on the mercy of friends. The floor in the Sixth Street house was mine again. The only job I could come up with was janitor for the Goodwill store. Every day I swept the floors and cleaned the bathrooms. I was told that if I stuck with it I might eventually get promoted to the job of putting the clothes on hangers.

John and I started spending time together. I didn't understand the complexities of putting a relationship together, and didn't bother to think it through very carefully (as was my habit). Every day after work I walked by his house so I could stop in and visit. One night I spent the night. Then the next night. Since I didn't have any place to live anyway, I moved in—which meant I brought my backpack over. So there I was, a member of the Fourth Street house, with John, Jay, and Kathy. I did it because I was broke. But still I felt a funny strangeness, like I didn't belong.

I wanted to contribute to the household, but had yet to make a paycheck, so I offered to pay rent for that month with sacks of bulk food—complete with instructions on how to use it—to keep the household food bills low. John and I went together to pick up the supplies. I had seriously overbought a few items, such as flour, beans, and rice. We drove his old truck to the beginning of the Homestake Creek road and skied the four miles into the cabin.

I sewed a harness for Sheela and we had her pull the food out on a sled. Her first practice of pulling the sled was pulling it empty into the cabins while we skied. On the way out she was loaded down with 25 pounds of food. She was a champ, and took to sledding like a natural.

I spent five weeks in town. By that time I had a few paychecks and it was starting to become obvious that living with John, Jay, and Kathy was not working out. Kathy was getting more and more pregnant. I wasn't skillful in helping in her house (I was too shy to ask what I should do), and John and I didn't know each other well enough to be living together. We had a fight. I decided to move back to Homestake Creek and quit my job.

On the day I left the house I had another one of those bad moments with money. I had paid 75 dollars for rent. But since I was leaving, even though it was sudden, Jay and Kathy told me to take the money back.

It was early in the morning, Jay and Kathy were still in bed and I was talking to them there. They said, "Take the money."

I refused. It seemed to me that I had made a commitment for the month in paying my money into the kitty that was a can on top of the piano.

They said, "Take it."

I said, "No."

They insisted. I insisted. Then I turned to leave. Past their bed, in a little sitting room, was the piano with the can of rent money on top. My hands reached up, as if drawn by an unknown force. I actually crawled up onto the piano seat, took my money from the can, and left the house ashamed. I should have either said, "Thanks," and taken the money, or insisted and not taken the money.

I had enough money for the rest of the winter now. There was a big hole in my head where understanding about money should have been. There was another hole where understanding about relationships should have been. These two things didn't make as much sense as carrying down the quakies or sweeping snow, so I couldn't find a way to begin thinking about them. I bought a few groceries and hiked back out the Homestake Creek. Ray nodded hello and I joined him sweeping the trails.

The snow was a soft blanket over my hurt feelings. Two days in my cabin and the softness of the wilderness was back in my heart. The snow covered hills brought me into the timeless moment of now. I resisted going into town as much as possible for the rest of the winter.

New Life

There was one big exception to my staying-out-of-town rule. Kathy was planning on having her baby at home, and Jay was going to be the midwife. There were no actual midwives in Leadville at that time. If you wanted to have a baby at home you had to do it all by yourself.

Kathy and Jay studied all the books that were available on home birth. I never questioned her choice. Natural people had been having babies for a million years before hospitals were invented. I was thrilled when she asked me to attend the birth and help.

Kathy wanted me to be in town one week before the baby was due so I wouldn't miss. I hiked out of Homestake Creek in plenty of time and moved in with some friends who had a spare room about a block away. John had taken off on a trip to California. The Goodwill Store let me work a few shifts, so I was able to make a little more money.

I'd been in town four days when Kathy went into labor. I rushed over to her house. My job was to hand her ice when her mouth got dry. Poor girl. I wanted to make sure I was doing my job right so I kept forcing ice on her. Finally, she gave me a look that would curd fresh milk. She was in transition; I backed off.

Once she started pushing, my job was to be the right side holder. She had another friend who was left side holder and Jay was the catcher. We helped brace her knees so she could be in a half sitting position on the bed while she pushed. In no time at all, effortless for me, there was a baby.

Who could believe that babies come into the world in exactly that way? God came down and touched our hands. The baby was perfect. Pink with a little black hair and dainty lips. There were plenty of other people to hold her so I never got to. I hovered to the side while Jay cleaned her up and wrapped her in a blanket. Then she snuggled into the arms of her mom. I marveled at the little crinkled face.

John got home from California the next day. As I was packing my bag to head back out to the cabins he came over to see me. He wasn't a guy who talked much. We sat in the living room and I filled in the blanks by asking him about his trip. It seemed that we weren't mad at each other any more. He stayed about an hour and then left.

Long Time Spring

The dogs and I hiked back to Homestake creek. I had a new lightness in my heart. The snow smiled upon me as I skied to my peaceful home.

I relaxed into the winter again. Occasionally, I worried over what I should do about John and sat up at night meditating on the problem. What was the deal with that? I didn't know that human beings, just like other animals, have little quirky things they have to do to make relationships happen. I sure didn't know what those quirky things were.

I did seem to know that I had to sit back and let John come to me. That letting go thing isn't prominent in my personality. I alternated between fuming and wondering. Ray and I swept the trails and played the baseball game. Snows came and sometimes there were sunny days. We watched as the snow lost its grip on the land.

In Sanskrit, the ancient language of the Hindus, the soul is called *atman*. That word means happiness, or bliss itself. Relaxing into the tiny world of the Homestake Creek cabins and the immense world of mountain snow allowed atman to rise to the surface. Days turned into months and the snow slowly sank.

Snow stays in Homestake Creek until late May. It piles up fast from the big snows, but melts down slowly. Towards the end of April, we'd had our fill of frozen white stuff. Time to start thinking about getting out of there.

Ray showed me how to make the driveway melt faster. Each afternoon we threw ash from our stoves out on the drifts. The black ashes would magnify the sun and melt the drifts faster. We also sprinkled sawdust from the sawing block. When we ran out of ash and sawdust, I dug down near the base of pine trees and collected pine needles to throw onto the reluctant drifts.

The driveway looked dirty and black, but we were ready to get out and drive the truck. One day, May 25th, we heard an engine. I sat on the hill by my cabin and watched a snowplow make its steady way up the Homestake Creek road.

A snowplow! The road was open!

I grabbed a shovel and heaved-to on the snow blocking the driveway. I was determined to get myself out now. The quarter-mile driveway took two days to shovel enough so that I could plow through with the four-wheel drive truck. What a thrill to be out on wheels again.

Slowly, the world turned green. Pasque flowers bloomed on the downward side of patches of snow. Coyotes stopped howling and birds started singing. The cats tumbled in the green meadows and the dogs shed their winter coats.

Housecleaning

Ray Kelley had asthma. Almost every night he would wake up, unable to breathe. During the winter in the mornings, while sweeping trails or having a little morning tea over at his house, he would tell me the nightly story. Exactly what time he woke up, how scary it was, how many times he had to take his inhaler, and how long it took for him to be able to breathe and get back to sleep.

I was absolutely no help to him. During the day he looked fine.

The doctor friend had looked Ray over and taken him down to Denver a couple of times, trying to figure out how to fix his asthma. But he didn't give him a prescription. Ray used an over-the-counter asthma inhaler.

Ray had been years in his tiny cabin with his cats. He kept it tidy, but it was very dirty inside from the accumulation of dust and cat hair. After spring had come and the days were sunny and warm I decided I was going to clean it out. I thought that living in there with all that cat dander and dust was making his asthma worse.

It took me a couple of days to convince him. First I asked gently, "Ray, I'd like to clean out your cabin."

"Oh no." He wasn't going to let that happen.

Finally I just told him, "Ray. I'm going to clean out your cabin. You have no choice. You might as well help."

So, we waited for a nice sunny day that looked like it would hold for a week, and proceeded to pull every single item that Ray owned out of the cabin. He had magazines and old clothes and everything you could imagine stacked in every corner. We pulled out the mattress, bed boards, and everything. The only thing left standing in his cabin was his little cook stove.

I went in there with a broom and started sweeping out the dust that had collected on the logs and up on the rafters above. It was toxic, old, killer dust. It fell on me in a poisonous cloud. After ten minutes, I came out and tied a bandana across my face and nose. I wouldn't let Ray go in. The dust was killing me. I was afraid what it might do to him. I had my own first asthma attack on that day and I have been allergic to cats ever since.

I got the first dust out of there, and then I filled a big bucket with hot soapy water, went in and scrubbed all the logs of the walls and ceiling. It was easy to reach since it was such a small cabin.

After the cabin was clean I didn't want to put all the dirty stuff back in. Ray was starting to get more into the spirit of spring cleaning, so we piled all his bedding, clothing, and every piece of rag from his cabin into the truck and headed down to the Laundromat in Vail.

We were a sight. Sitting there in the huge, clean, rich Laundromat. Vail was a new ski area town where the beautiful people lived their beautiful lives. But there we were, Ray with his old hat, stooped shoulders, and bony knees pressing against his cleanest pair of pants as he sat in the chair waiting for it to all be over. Me, dusty black braid hanging to the middle of my back, scratched wire-rimmed glasses on my face, stuffing the washing machines full of dirty gray rags and clothes.

It took two washings through the machines to turn the material into an acceptable shade of gray. Some things fell apart to threads. I think dirt was the only thing holding them together. We were in a cleaning frenzy.

Vail is a condominium ski resort town. Homestake Creek was between Vail and Leadville on Highway 24. We were actually closer to Vail than to Leadville for shopping. Every time we went to Vail, about four times a year, Ray would tell me about the old days. "I knew this valley when it was just a sheep camp," he would say. "And look at it now." We would shake our heads sadly at the thick huddle of condominiums.

Out on the highway driving home, every single time, he would point to a gully surrounded by fancy storefronts, and say, "That's where the sheep camp would sit, Old Man Miller and his dogs. Right there." Ray would shake his head, rub his whiskered chin and tisk his tongue. "And look at it now."

The valley was nothing but rows of condominiums filling the horizon.

"When the enemy comes," Ray would say, "they're going to use Vail as barracks."

I would always laugh and reply, "Ray, the enemy is already here."

We both shook our heads and drove on until we reached the familiar horizon of the Continental Divide and our valley. When we arrived home we put everything back in his cabin. Ray's asthma got better instantly because he wasn't breathing all that cat dander. He started sleeping through the night.

I, on the other hand, remain allergic to cats and plagued with asthma to this day.

Chapter Thirteen

Working the Claim

Life on Homestake Creek was simple. Winters were relaxed because there was nothing to do but sweep the trails. Summers were relaxed because it was so warm and comfortable.

I wrote regular letters to my parents and my grandmother. When Grandma wrote back she sometimes stuck a five-dollar bill into the envelope with the letter. Those five-dollar bills were my main income. Spring had come now and there seemed no need for money of any sort. We all basked in the sun; four-legged and two-legged.

I wasn't completely lazy, however, because Ray and I had work to do. We needed to get in wood for the next winter, and we needed to work the claim.

A mining claim isn't legal private property out in the forest. The land is owned temporarily. Many of the laws have changed now, but years ago anyone could go out, find sign of mineral and claim land for mining. You could live on the land for free as long as you followed a few rules. A certain amount of paperwork was involved, each year, and you had to do some work on the claim to prove that it was a working concern. For Ray's claim, we needed to do a hundred dollars worth of work each year.

Each summer Ray and I did our improvements. The first summer we worked on the middle claim. The second summer we patched up the roof of the garage. After making our improvements we drove down to the ranger station in the town of Eagle to report what we'd done.

Cleaning out the middle claim was our first job. This was my opportunity to get a good look at the work this one man had done with the hope of striking it big. The middle claim was up a rocky slope to the northwest of the cabins. A tunnel was blasted straight into the sheer rock of the mountain, twenty feet deep, and the height and width of a small man. Ray could stand up in it. My head hit the top unless I stooped over slightly.

When Ray was a young man he loved to blast dynamite. This became a little scary after he got older. His dynamite technique was to set the charges, and then run off until it blew. As time progressed his running abilities got weaker, and the mines got deeper, a dangerous combination.

For years he worked the mines by himself, blasting and then shoveling out the broken rocks—looking for something shiny. His geological know-how pretty much centered on the fact that good rock would be shiny.

For our job of cleaning out the middle claim we had a wheelbarrow, a pick, and two shovels. The mine hadn't been worked for five years and a lot of rock had caved in around the mouth of the tunnel. Ray didn't think I should work inside the tunnel. That would be too dangerous for a little girl. We shoveled rock from the mouth of the cave into the wheelbarrow and dumped it over the lip of the slag pile. We ate our lunch up at the "jobsite." Ray wore his miner's hard hat. I wore work gloves. We did this for two days, until Ray declared it was a hundred dollars worth of work. Next day we drove down to Eagle and reported our job to the Forest Service.

Down at the Forest Service office they told me pieces of the true story about Ray's mining claim. I never understood exactly, but I think there was no need for us to do our hundred dollars worth of work any more. A deal had already been made concerning the ownership of Ray's land.

A couple of years before I arrived on Homestake Creek, Ray was delivered into a Forest Service meeting and coerced into signing papers that gave him the right to keep the mining claims with no more work requirements for as long as he lived. As soon as he was gone the claims would revert back to the Forest Service.

He didn't like the agreement and was looking for a way to get the mine back to regular mining claim status. He was hoping I could help. Ray had worked hard at building his cabins.

"These are my cabins, Coni," he told me as we drove home from Eagle. "And we can't let the Forest Service take them away after I'm gone."

"They can't do that, can they, Ray?" I asked. I wasn't any good at understanding political maneuverings.

"They want to build a campground. Tear down the cabins and put in a campground. There are enough campgrounds." He hunched down close to the wheel as he drove, pushing his lower dentures in and out with his jaw. "I don't know what will happen to the kitties. They can't go wild. They'll never make it in the wild."

I was silent as we drove. We were talking about what would happen when Ray Kelley was gone. But he had always been there. Wouldn't he always be there?

He asked me if I would sign papers to make me a legal partner in the claim. I resisted the idea.

Ray had quite a few part-time friends who had known him for years before I showed up on the mining claim: the doctor, Gary Fishback, and all the people from the Colorado Mountain Club. They came occasionally to visit, and we treated each other with thinly-disguised suspicion. I wanted them to go away. I'm sure they wanted me to go away. They thought I was taking advantage of Ray by living out in his cabins.

I thought this was a pretty unfair judgment. Sure these old friends had known him longer, and they had lots of money and brought him treats from the store. But, in my opinion, I had something better than that. I had time to give, and I spent time with him summer and winter. A human being with time is as least as important as an occasional donut.

I have this same opinion about raising kids. I'm not a proponent of "quality time." I think adults who are raising children should have long, drawn-out lengths of time to just hang around without any particular agenda. Lots of relaxed attention, doing nothing, drawn out into all the minutes of the day. That's the food that feeds a child's soul. Childhood is made of the long lazy days of summer and short bursts of excited sledding in winter. So is friendship.

That was my gift to Ray—I just hung out. His friends valued my gift as little as a parent's time is valued with their children today. We were having a generational conflict. I didn't respect them. They didn't respect me. Ray didn't care. He liked us all.

I preferred to keep the conflict as silent as possible. I was afraid that signing papers to be a partner on the claim would fuel the idea that I was trying to take advantage of Ray. I didn't want the silent battle to go into open heat.

He begged me and begged me, however, and finally I agreed. What a surprise when I saw the paper he wanted me to sign. It had about fifty names on it. I signed on the bottom line and Ray was happy as could be.

The other fifty names were every single person Ray had met over the past ten years. He was hoping that one of them would know how to save the claim. It was a game of numbers if nothing else.

The Mines

I was now a partner in a going concern, even though, as far as I could tell, the partnership and the concern had no basis in legal reality. But Ray was happy. In the past Ray's mine had been his dream of making it big. He had put in a tremendous amount of work to make that dream a reality. Each summer, while working for the railroad, Ray had spent his vacation working his mines under the tutelage of the old miners who lived out on the creek. Once he retired he went to work full time.

He had three claims staked out on the mountainside. The lower claim was where we lived, then there was the middle claim to the northwest of the cabin, and the upper claim straight up the hill to the west of the cabins. On the lower claim he blasted a shaft straight down into the earth.

"Look Coni," he would say, pointing up the hill at a ridge of rock behind the cabins. "That's the Iron Dyke. It's full of mineral." Then he'd pull his hat off his head, wipe the sweat from his brow, and give me a knowing nod. It was all there, shiny mineral, right in that Iron Dyke.

The shaft he had blasted on the lower claim was deep. I couldn't see its complete glory because it was filled with water. Ray told me about blasting the hole. His system was: climb down the ladder, set the dynamite, scurry up the ladder as fast as he could, pull the ladder out of the hole, run behind a rock outcropping and hold his ears until it blasted. When the smoke cleared he lowered the ladder back into the hole, climbed back down and lifted out broken rock with a bucket.

He got the shaft deep enough to hit water, and that caused all sorts of problems. So he bought himself a compressor. Now he had to pump out the water, blast the hole, pump water again and then climb down and bucket up the rocks.

The day he quit the mine on the lower claim was the day he was caught by the blast before he could pull up the ladder. It was a close call and a sign that he was getting too slow to make the ever-increasing climb out of the shaft.

There was one day before that, "the exciting day," when he set the charge, blew the blast, climbed down and found a giant shiny rock. He was certain he had hit the big time. He hauled his find up only to discover it glittered even more gloriously in the sunshine. He was so excited he drove immediately to Denver to get it checked out. He had found something!

Turned out it was an iron rock. Not the gold he had hoped for, but it did prove that the Iron Dyke was truly an Iron Dyke. He didn't have the iron rock any more. I think it was down in Denver at the Doctor's house. But, be it known to all, that the Iron Dyke is an excellent piece of mining property, and Ray once found a shiny rock on a very exciting day. This is important stuff for storytelling on long winters' nights.

The Upper Claim

The upper claim was a magical place. To get there you followed a faint trail up through the trees behind Ray's cabin. The trail took three switchbacks, then opened into a flat, grassy meadow surrounded by Quaking Aspen. There was no mineshaft on the upper claim, but Ray had built a cabin up there out of one hundred percent Quakie logs. It was the neatest, cleanest cabin of all. He used green quakies for the walls and they had cured into giant incense sticks. I loved to run my fingers along the white powder on the Quakie bark, inhaling the perfume.

Aspen powder is a fine white powder that forms on the bark of Quaking Aspen. It has a rich, clean smell and my books said the Indians used it for insect repellant. It works great.

Outside the upper-claim cabin was a small stream of water (not reliable all year) and a tiny lean-to outhouse. Only two sides of the outhouse had been built and it covered a shallow hole that was mostly overgrown with grass. You could sit there and look right out to the meadow while you did your business. No need for a door in the privy at the upper-claim.

Celebrity

Getting in wood was our biggest job for the summer. This year I had plenty of time to carry quakies off the hillside. We hiked up and down the trail as a regular occupation, carrying in two sticks at a time.

Ray had this one particular habit. It was his opinion that pants would bind one's legs when hiking up steep hills. He was right, of course.

Go ahead and try it out. You'll see. Take a hike up a hot steep hill. The material of your pants will grab and pull at your knees with each step. The hotter the day, the more the pants pull, and that slight pull is enough to tire a guy out when hauling in Quakies.

The logical solution is to wear shorts, but Ray was from a generation very different than ours. He didn't have any shorts; he didn't wear shorts. As a matter of fact, he didn't always wear underwear. I never got the story on the underwear, but perhaps they bound something up too.

On a hot day, as the temperature rose, Ray would take his pants off, fold them nice and neat, and place them on a rock. Then he'd hike up the mountain, get his sticks and hike back down the mountain again. His legs were a deep brown from the sun. Because he was a small man his T-shirts hung rather low on his body, making this not such a dramatic sight as could be imagined. I didn't care one way or the other. He was comfortable, I was comfortable—that was all that mattered.

Ray had this one favorite rock where he liked to put his pants. It was a little ways up the mountain, and there was a reason for this too. He would start gathering sticks early in the morning when it was cool. As the sun rose in the sky the heat would rise. Ray would usually start feeling the heat on the second trip *up* the mountain. And this particular rock was so nice and handy. It was flat and squarish, the perfect thing to hold pants until the day's work was done.

On this particular day we had each taken a couple trips up the mountain for a few sticks. We were sitting in the sun near the cabins eating our lunch. Ray still didn't have his pants on, because why bother going halfway up the mountain to get his pants just for a lunch break? I was in my shorts. We heard an engine noise on the breeze and looked out across the meadow to the Homestake Creek road. We watched as this van stopped in the middle of the road. Four men piled out of the van and stood there, looking and pointing in our direction. Then they jumped back in the van, turned around and headed back down the road towards the mining claim driveway. The "Danger! Mining Claim! Blasting! Keep Out!" signs didn't even slow them down. We heard the engine tone as it curved up the driveway towards us.

Ray Kelley and I looked at each other, "They're coming here."

Ray didn't have any pants on, so he scurried away to retrieve them. I went over to the garage to see who the intruders might be. Turned out they were from Channel Nine News down in Denver. Someone had told them about this guy who lived up on a mining claim and they wanted to do one of their personal news stories on him.

They kept asking me, "Where is the guy who lives here?" I stalled. Ray didn't seem to be coming back too quickly. I thought he might be hiding out. I was certainly not about to tell them that he was off looking for his pants. I tried to make small talk to fill the time. The cameramen acted suspicious.

Finally Ray came back and I told him what was going on. They wanted to film him. Ray wagged his head and clicked his tongue; that would be foolish. I told Ray, "Oh go ahead and do it."

He worried about his cats, then he worried about the dogs, then he worried about why they would want to do it at all. But he finally agreed to be a news story and the crew set to work getting their cameras out of the van.

As soon as Ray got in front of the camera, he turned on. He talked nonstop while he showed the cabins and got his hard hat to head for the mine. He was a miner, after all, so we had to show the mine. Ray sprinted up the hill to the middle claim. That young camera crew huffed along behind the skinny old man. They wouldn't take any pictures of me, of course, and seemed quite disappointed that I was there at all. I wasn't interesting because I wasn't an old man living all by himself on a mining claim. I was ruining their story just being there.

They photographed Ray as he walked up the hill to the mine, with Levi and Sheila both running along with him and getting into the pictures. They all got to be on TV.

Ray thought it was unfair that the dogs got in the picture. He made the cameraman take pictures of the cats. But I guess the cats weren't very TV worthy, so they didn't make the cut. It was all very unfair, but we should at least feel fortunate that Ray Kelley had his pants on.

Of course, we never saw it on TV. The closest TV was over ten miles away and we never thought to go looking for one. We were lucky at this point to know who was president. But quite a few of my friends told me, later, that they had seen it. First they recognized the dogs, and then they realized the man was Ray. We were a little bit famous and we were a little bit proud.

Work

You may think from all these stories that I was a very industrious person: carrying wood, working the claim, long hikes, one minute behind the cameras of fame. But truly, I was as lazy as the day I was born. Work activity took up a small portion of my time. Mostly, I kicked back and did nothing. Winters were lazy because there was nothing to do, and summers were lazy because they were comfortable and warm.

Recently I read a report from anthropologists on studies they have done on native hunter-gatherer people. Far from our conventional idea that primitive people lived gruesome, hard, savage lives, the researchers have found that they were comfortable and relaxed. Native humans worked only a few hours a day. The rest of the time was spent eating, talking and playing with one another. They laughed a lot over their own gossip.

My experience tells me that this must be true. When I am living without modern pressures, the urge to work comes upon me for only short periods each day. The rest of the time is spent in contentment making.

Chapter Fourteen

How to Flute a Moose

Occasionally, I would still go to town. It was summer now, and me being a partner on the claim and all, Ray let me use his truck. My hitchhiking days were over. This meant that I could actually drive in to Leadville and back out to Homestake Creek in the same day. Quite a luxury.

I would stop by to visit John occasionally and we were becoming better friends. He came and visited me a couple of times. This put me into a whole new group in Leadville. I liked hanging out with John, Tim, and Courtney. Their passion was climbing to the very tip-top of the highest mountains.

Leadville itself is 10,000 feet in altitude. The second step of the courthouse measures in at two miles high, but that's nothing compared to the mountains of the Continental Divide. The town sits in a wide open plain dominated by the slopes of Mount Massive and the towering peak of Mount Elbert which, at 14,433 feet, is the highest peak in Colorado.

One night there was a great full moon and a clear sky. I was in town visiting. John had moved out of the house with Jay and Kathy, now that the baby was there, and he was sharing an old house with Tim and Courtney. We are sitting up late, listening to music (didn't even need batteries) and we suddenly decided to climb Mount Massive. We got together a few supplies, piled into Courtney's car and drove as far as we could up the mountain. By the time we started hiking it was two o'clock in the morning. Our goal was to be at the very top of the mountain as the sun came up.

The moonlight was bright enough that we didn't need flashlights. We climbed hard for four hours. It was brutal going in the high altitude air, climbing and climbing, forcing one leg after the other in front of me up the steep slope. The moonlight turned to early morning haze, and I could tell that the sun was getting ready to come up.

Ridge after ridge fooled me into thinking it was the top of the mountain. But finally I mounted one large ridge and could see the true top, still a long ways up. The morning was getting brighter. I couldn't speed up enough to make it. But John had these big, long legs. He left the rest of us behind and sped up the mountain. I watched his legs eat up the slope as he climbed. I scrambled slowly behind. He was sitting on top of the highest peak as the first shafts of sunlight slipped from the east. I made it up about twenty minutes later. We sat there and watched tongues of sun lick the world. Shadows slowly sunk into the canyons, becoming smaller and smaller until daylight claimed the land.

I stood on top of the highest rock and turned, looking down on an alien world below me. The earth was a vast crinkled horizon. There were no trees, or flowers, or paths. Trees were a blue fuzz on cracked ridges, becoming bluer and bluer in the distance until they were nothing. Who could believe that this was the same planet I had crawled around on my whole life? I saw folds of geology in every direction. The town of Leadville was an unidentifiable speck in one of those folds.

The Forest Service puts sealed metal boxes on top of high summits. Inside is a journal so the people who have climbed the mountains can write their names. We opened the box and read through the names of the people who had been here before us. Then Tim signed the book, "Frank and Friends were here."

Frank was this imaginary character who had been invented by Tim. Instead of saying, "We're just fucking around," he would say, "We're just franking around." Frank became this invisible friend who lived with the group. So if you ever climb a mountain and read the journal and find an entry from "Frank and Friends" you will know that it was either Tim,

Courtney, John, me, or anyone who ever knew us or climbed a mountain with us and decided to join Frank's crew.

We climbed several "fourteeners" that summer, including Mount of the Holy Cross. I really enjoyed that climb because access to the trailhead is up the Homestake Creek road. Everyone came and visited my home to pick me up for the climb.

That hike was long, but not too steep, as we took two days for the assent and camped at an area over 12,000 feet high. The top of the mountain was a massive slope. We reached the summit and strolled over to the edge where the mountain dropped off suddenly at our feet, down into the crevasse that holds the cross of snow that gives the mountain its name.

As we stood there another group of hikers came up to us. We had seen this group down at the base of the mountain and had ignored them as proper "I-wish-it-was-only-me" mountain etiquette dictated. But then one guy from this group walks right up to me and asks, "Are you Connie Delaney?"

Shocked I just stood there. "What?" Here I was over 14,000 feet high and some guy knows my name! What?

Turns out he had been one class below me at Wheatridge High School, and he remembered me. I don't know what it is. Maybe I have a strange face or something. Maybe it's the way I act. People seem to always remember me. I'm not as invisible as I think.

We signed "Frank and friends were here" in the box on top of Mount of the Holy Cross and made our way down. I carried away a heightened sense of paranoia!

In the Real Wilderness

I visited town quite a bit that summer. I sold some pieces of embroidery and helped a friend manage his sandwich shop while he was off with the

National Guard one week. During one of my visits, Levi disappeared. She was just gone and I never found out what happened to her.

A short time after that John asked me to go on a long backpacking trip with him. His goal was to spend as much time as possible out in the real wilderness area of no roads, and go as far as possible. He was attracted by the Selway-Bitterroot and River of No Return Wilderness areas in Central Idaho and South-West Montana. This part of the country is the biggest chunk of wilderness area in the continental United States. Only Alaska has more wilderness. Perfect for us.

We caught a ride with Tim, who was going as far as Stanley. It took two days to get to Idaho. The second night we camped near the headwaters of the Salmon River out of Stanley, Idaho. John decided to go fishing, so he crossed the river over to the other bank and was sitting there with his pole. Tim and I hung out on the bank on our side.

I saw a movement in the water, "What is that?"

I focused and realized I was looking at the biggest fish I had ever seen. It was sitting almost still. Floating in an eddy of water.

Tim took one look and declared, "I'm getting that fish!"

"Great!" I thought. He didn't have a fishing pole. He didn't have anything. He was sitting there in his shorts, not even wearing a shirt. Tim got down and crept along the sand on his belly; he didn't want the fish to see him. It was "man the hunter" in all his glory. Tim slithered right up to the water. Then, slap! He grabbed the fish and threw it up on the bank.

The fish flopped on the sand and Tim yelled across the stream to John, "I caught a fish! I caught a fish!"

He had caught himself a Salmon. It was a female who had already spawned so she was all depleted, but Tim was still a hero. He had caught a fish with his bare hands. We had fresh, hand-caught fish for dinner that night.

John once caught a fish with his bare hands too. This was years later when we were living up in Idaho. We were going fishing at a high mountain lake. This lake was unique because in the fifties it had been stocked with fish. Fish couldn't get out the small outlet, so these stocked fish lived in this lake and grew and multiplied. Very few people go fishing there because you have to hike in about 12 miles. I'm not telling you exactly where the lake is because it is best kept a secret.

We were hiking up to the lake. It was early spring, during a big run-off year. The outlet from the lake was running deep across the trail. I heard a strange flapping and said, "Look, John. There is a fish."

A huge lake trout had been washed down the creek and was flopping in the shallow water.

So John-the-hunter threw down his backpack, jumped over, grabbed that fish out of the water, and held it up with man-caught-fish-with-his-bare-hands triumphant look on his face. I took a picture of him. So John and Tim have both caught live fish with their bare hands. Knowing the whole story, it's not all that great because both fish were begging to caught, but still, they did it. So there is proof that human beings can catch fish with their bare hands.

To the Bitterroot Valley

Tim left us in Stanley, Idaho. John and I hitched the rest of the way up to Hamilton, Montana, and into Blodget canyon. I was used to the massive mountains of Colorado and had never seen anything like this slice of low-land rock. It looked like a giant knife had cut a piece of pie out of the mountain. North of Blodget were two more canyons that looked like the same knife had severed them. The setting sun shone on the sidewalls of the cliffs, like a paintbrush had swiped them with gold.

We wanted to get as far into the wilderness as possible before camping, so we divvied up the food, put it in our backpacks, and hefted them upon our shoulders. The shoulder straps cut into my skin like that knife going through the rock to cut Blodget canyon. John, honestly, took 20 more than me, but I could barely move my knees as I struggled under the weight. I forced myself to remain upright. We hiked into the slice of golden sun on the cliffs.

Sheela carried all her food in a doggy backpack that I had sewn on a treadle sewing machine. She carried some of our food too. Her back sagged from the weight, but she still gave us a happy dog-grin as we marched up the trail.

We hiked for ten days and went over a hundred miles.

How to Flute a Moose

In my pack was my silver flute. I had made a little travel sack for it so I could bring it along without having to carry the heavy case. Even though the flute added extra weight to my pack, I loved to carry it to remote lakes and play against the echoes from the cliffs. A lake and a cliff make a perfect amphitheater for a person with a flute.

After three days of hiking we got to Hidden Lake. It was a long, thin lake down in a wooded slice of the mountains. The middle of the lake was the dark blue of deep water. John took off on a hike. He wanted to get up high and look down. I was too tired to go any further, so I sat by the bank and played my flute. As I played I noticed a brown speck out in the middle of the lake. The speck got closer and closer, and turned into a moose. It dog-paddled diligently towards me, head tilted up out of the water against the weight of flat-round antlers, blowing air from its giant nostrils, until it came to the end of the deep water. He climbed the bank near the shore where I sat, his knobby knees straining to pull that huge body from the water. I kept the flute song going, over and over, not daring to stop.

The moose stood and looked at me, water dripping in sheets from the long hairs on its chest. Then, suddenly, he shook himself all over like a big dog—one of those shakes that start at the nose and shimmer down the sides of the animal, ending with the last drops of water flipping off its tail.

His ears flapped side to side from the effort of sending that shake down his tremendous body.

Laughter stopped my flute song. The moose gave me an empty look and slipped back into the water.

Food

We didn't want to carry an extra ounce of weight, so our food was pre-measured exactly for each day. Dinner was rice, lentils, and dried vegetables. Lunch was crackers and cheese, breakfast, granola and dried milk. That's it.

We thought we were the cleverest people with our food and our economy and all our measuring and counting our crackers. Then halfway through the trip we met this fellow who was packing along carrying a guitar.

We said hello, with curiosity. Our conversation quickly turned to weight and economy in backpacking. He was carrying a guitar! How did he manage that? We told him about our exact food calculations. He answered back telling us how smart *he* was with his food.

Out of his backpack he pulled a gun. John and I stepped back looking for a getaway. This guy's food strategy was to shoot squirrels and eat them! Too strange for us! We didn't tell him which direction we were going and made sure we were a considerable way off before we camped that night. That fellow seemed nice enough, but he was a little too strange. If you ever wonder where all the squirrels in the Selway-Bitterroot have gone that might be the place to start looking.

The next day we were hiking along and ran across a Forest Ranger riding a horse. She told us how to find the wilderness ranger station and invited us over. At this Ranger Station we were fed the most delicious meal ever cooked on the face of planet earth. The rangers live 20 miles from any road. They had to bring all their supplies in with horses, so they grew the most wonderful garden. She let us eat anything we wanted out of that garden. We ate salad, potatoes, creamy sauces, and every wonderful possible thing that could be eaten by vegetarians. Those poor rangers must have been afraid they were going to have to carry us from their house. True hunger lets you taste true food. Mmmm. Was that good!

That was the moment I decided I wanted to grow my own gardens.

We came out of our backpacking trip on the other side of the Bitterroot Mountains. We had gone up over the mountains and down, and then followed the Selway River to its mouth. We cleaned ourselves up at the commercial campground there and hitchhiked back to Colorado. John went back to work at the mine. I stayed with him a few weeks while I waited tables to make a little money. Then I headed back to Homestake Creek with my small earnings.

It had been a long time ago when it took $500 in my pocket to make me feel safe. Now it seemed to me that as long as I had $65 I had everything. My little cabin was happy to see me. Ray nodded his head and clicked his teeth. Looked like we were ready for winter.

Coming Snows

Come winter, John decided he was tired of working at the mine and he quit. I guess I was a bad influence on him. He moved onto the mining claim with me.

My little cabin was too small for John. He couldn't stand up in it. So we moved into the big cabin. This was luxury, two whole rooms with a full-height ceiling. One room was a kitchen and the other room was the bedroom.

In this spacious kitchen, we had an actual adult-size wood stove. I could stand up straight while I cooked on it. It was here that I learned how to make corn tortillas and tofu.

The snows came in and blanketed us with their forgiveness. We played the baseball game, swept the walks, read books and had an occasional visit from our skiing friends in Leadville. Occasionally, the Colorado Mountain Club came up and had to cram into the little cabin because we were taking up the bigger dwelling.

One difference in having a companion in my cabin with me was that I had a ski partner. One day we decided to see how far we could get up the Homestake Creek road.

John and I got up early in the morning, packed our lunch, and took off skiing. It was warm that day and the snow was wet. Lots of snowmobiles had gone up the road since the last snow so we were skiing on packed ice.

Four miles up Homestake Creek we turned right onto the road that led to the ridge overlooking the Mount of the Holy Cross. I knew I could never make it to the top of the ridge but skied bravely on. I'm sure I went too far for my ability. By the time we turned around, I was exhausted and still had a long trip home.

The road down was steep. John still had lots of energy so he headed down before me. The icy snowmobile trail was killer fast. I watched as he raced down the hill and disappeared from sight. Slowly, I began my shaky snowplow descent. I was afraid to let myself go too fast because I couldn't make the curves with my wooden skis.

I inched down. My legs were shaking from holding back on the ice of the snowmobile trail. Finally, I decided to get up on the unsmashed snow on the side of the road, a thin band that the snowmobiles had ignored. Problem was, this put me within a few inches of the side of the mountain that fell off into space. I was okay around the first switchback, but found myself gaining speed on the straightaway that followed. I couldn't snowplow because there was no room to spread my skis. Faster and faster I flew until I spilled off the side, headfirst into space.

The only thing that saved me was my right ski catching on a bush at the top of the cliff. I hung upside-down, little tufts of snow falling from the bush onto my head. John was long gone off the mountain—no telling how long until he might come back for me. Dusk was beginning to fall. I hung there, still, not moving, upside down on the cliff, caught by one ski. The other foot dangled loose against the cliff. My stocking hat was still on my head, gloved hands clutching my poles. Hanging and panting.

I hung there just taking stock. This was not the best of all situations. I was kind of mad, blaming it on John. Best not to move until I calmed.

After awhile I tested my ski's hold on the bush and found it to be stable. I tossed my poles up to the road, and did an upside-down sit-up until I could touch my feet. I held onto the bush and undid my skis. First the loose one. Then, holding onto the bush, I undid the one that held me to land. I slid up through the snow to the road, tucked my skis and poles under my arms and hiked down the snowmobile trail. Occasionally, one leg would fall through the crust. When I got to where the road was less steep I put the skis on again and skied until I met John just beginning to come back up. "What took you so long?"

Apparently, I was less skilled in birth control than I was in skiing steep slopes. I got pregnant in February of that year. I don't think John was too happy about this turn of events.

It never occurred to me that being pregnant might change my life. Natural people had been pregnant since the dawn of time. The Indians did it and didn't have to stop being Indians just to have a baby. They lived out in tipis. Joe and Bev had lived out in a tipi with their baby. Having a baby was going to be so easy for me; I didn't give it a second thought.

We stayed at Homestake the whole winter. Each night the moon came up 43 minutes later. Snows built up deep and then started to sink. In the spring we threw ashes onto the snow covering the driveway, and finally got the truck out. When the hillsides were bare Ray and I started carrying down sticks for the next year. John went to get firewood with the truck and a chainsaw.

My anthropological research was taking a new turn.

Chapter Fifteen

How Life Finds You

My pregnancy was a disturbance to my family. At first, I made a defiant stand declaring, even to my grandmother, that John and I were not going to get married. I couldn't understand what getting married would have to do with anything. After awhile, though, we relented and started calling ourselves married. Common Law marriage rules in Colorado made this actually legal. My grandmother sent me a nice "modern" wedding outfit: silky white pants and a matching top. One day I put on the outfit, held some flowers, stood by a bush in Courtney's yard and had my picture taken. We sent a copy of my wedding photo to Grandma and she felt a lot better.

As summer came back to our mountain world it became obvious that we needed to do something to make some money. Pure, natural people like us didn't like working underground in mines or inside restaurants. We wanted to work outside. We also wanted to go on another backpack trip, so John and I decided to try picking apples up in Washington State.

The question was how to get up north. One day we were driving through Leadville in John's truck and we saw a "For Sale" sign on a cool little blue car sitting behind a house.

John said, "That's a Volvo. Volvos are really good cars." It was a 1963 wagon.

We bought it with the last of John's money. All we had was enough for gas, but that was all we needed. We packed ourselves into the Volvo and headed north. We stopped in Idaho and went on a long backpacking trip. Me, with my growing belly and all.

We got up to Washington a couple of weeks before the picking season began and got ourselves onto a crew. Of course they thought I was crazy because I was eight months pregnant at this time. That didn't matter to me. I kept climbing up the ladder and picking the apples. I'll admit I didn't pick as many apples as everybody else, but I climbed up the ladder and picked as many apples as I could.

I never considered going to the hospital for labor and birth. My plan was to have the baby at home. I had been studying up on natural childbirth and felt ready. Kathy had done it with only Jay and two friends to help, I didn't see why I couldn't do the same thing. It was beginning to look like home was going to be the apple orchard, so we started asking around for a midwife. Finally, at another camp, we found a gal named Sarah who said she would come and help deliver the baby. Perfect.

One day, while the crews were off picking and I was in my picker's cabin alone, my water broke. I sent messages out to the crews for John to come home and called down to the other camp where Sarah was living. She rushed up to my cabin and helped me settle in. I had what you would call a clockwork labor. It was eight hours, transition came at the exact right time, and the birth was quite simple.

I had read that the most important thing was to relax your hands and relax your lips during contractions. I think this is the big secret in having a baby: don't worry about it. Relax your hands, relax your lips and let it happen all by itself. The most helpful thing I studied was a book written by midwives at a commune called The Ranch. This book was called *Spiritual Midwifery* and was full of very personal stories of ladies having babies. I learn best through stories, and these stories taught me. That's the way to teach young women about having babies. Tell them good stories.

So there was our baby. We decided to name him Jesse. We also wanted to name him after Ray, so he was Jesse Ray Skriletz.

Suddenly, I had this baby and I slowly began to catch onto the fact that I had no clue what to do, or what was going on. Up to that point I thought I was smart. Now that was over. My whole pregnancy I had been studying about how to have the baby, how to have a home birth. Never for one second did I consider that I had to do any sort of studying about what to do with the baby once I actually got it.

My mom drove up to Washington to visit and help. I was grateful. She showed me how to get a burp out of him, the best way to fold a diaper (yes, we used cloth diapers), and how to give him a bath without drowning him. Kathy and baby Thankful also came to help. I don't know what I would have done without the assistance of these women.

Once again, I didn't know that I was being natural by not knowing the answer to life. For two million years experienced women have shown new mothers how to take care of babies. That's what happened for me too. Keep up the good work, girls!

John finished up the season picking the apples. I stayed in the cabin and took care of Jesse. As soon as the season was up, we headed back to Colorado.

I was amazed at how exhausted I was, and useless. I couldn't do anything. I couldn't drive because I had to hold the baby (this was before carseat days or seatbelt laws). All I could manage to do was hold him, nurse him, and occasionally try to get some sleep. Jesse did not sleep well, especially on the trip. It was a long drive back to Leadville.

How Life Finds You

By the time we got back to the Colorado Mountains we were exhausted. We didn't have any plans, so we moved back into the big cabin. The first winter snows were starting to fly. I had reached a totally unplanned part of my life, and was just winging it. We installed a wood stove in the bedroom. The cook stove that was in the kitchen took too long to heat and it did not hold a fire for any length of time at night. We felt the baby would need quicker heat, especially since he got up so many times to feed.

I wasn't worried about having a baby on Homestake Creek. He seemed healthy—if loud enthusiastic crying was a sign of strong health. Bev and Joe had their baby out here in a tipi! We were in a cabin. I felt safe. The road was still opened. No problem for now.

John and I had the double bed in the corner, and I made a makeshift crib for Jesse nearer to the stove. I stayed in the cabin. John got a temporary carpenter job in Leadville and stayed in town when he was working, so I was by myself. Most of the time, when John was gone, I would keep Jesse in bed with me at night to make sure he was warm and so I didn't have to get up in the cold when he cried to be fed.

I was reading lots of books about the perfect ways to raise perfect babies, so I was concerned about a number of things. Number one was the fact that babies had to sleep lying on their stomachs. This was because they might spit up while sleeping and choke themselves. This was common knowledge at the time. Number two was that you shouldn't sleep in the same bed with a tiny baby because you might roll over on them and suffocate them in your sleep. I was very careful to give Jesse plenty of room when we shared a bed, just in case I should happen to actually get to sleep.

There were other, less critical concerns. Some books said that sleeping with a baby was good, because it made them feel snuggly and loved. Others said it would only spoil the child and make him dependent. Some books said you should let a baby cry and should keep him on a feeding schedule. Other books said that wasn't important. Traditional wisdom said babies should be nice and fat to be healthy and well-fed. My natural food gurus said fat was not good. Fat babies will become fat adults.

Jesse wasn't fat, and now, at six weeks old, he had colic, especially in the evening. I spent hours holding him over my shoulder and patting his back. My back and arms hurt. I felt like I hadn't slept once since the day he was born. My visions about having a natural baby didn't seem to be working out. I was frazzled and confused. There seemed to be a big piece missing in the puzzle of my Back to Eden experience, and I didn't know what it was.

I was glad when John came home that evening. They were waiting for some walls to arrive for the house they were building. The contractors had messed up in their timing, so he had a few days off. We had dinner and went to bed.

Jesse kept fussing even though he was snuggled up in bed with us. Maybe it was because there was suddenly someone new in the bed. Maybe he felt my worry that John would roll over on him. Finally, I decided that since he was fussing anyway he could sleep in his own bed. I knew I would be up a few times in the night to feed him and could keep the fire going and the cabin warm.

I tucked the baby into his blankets and slipped an extra one on him to keep him warm. I stoked the fire and banked it down low. It would keep the cabin warm for a good five hours. Jesse kept fussing and crying in his bed, sometimes sucking loudly on his fingers, sometimes crying out loud. He was fed, and his diaper was dry, so I knew there was nothing I could do to make him sleep. I let him cry.

I was tired, exhausted. John and I lay in bed, tossing, drifting off to sleep and waking back up again as Jesse cried himself to sleep. It was the longest time until he was quiet. I fell into a deep, deep, comatose, dreamless sleep.

I woke from this sleep as if coming out a thick, black tunnel. Grey light from a cloudy morning filled the cabin. I knew immediately that something was wrong. Just the fact that I had slept meant something was wrong. I leapt from bed and checked the crib. Jesse was dead.

I could tell in a second, in an instant, that there was no life in my baby.

I sat down hard on the floor. John woke, came over and looked. He knew too. I wouldn't touch Jesse. The look was all I needed. I got my coat and went outside and sat on the hill to the east of the house.

I sat there.

A thin dry snow was part of the sky. It wasn't really falling, but hanging in suspended motion. My mind was like the snow. It didn't have anything to think so it hung suspended.

John joined me on the hill. I don't think we talked.

I saw this little vision that my baby was like a fish. Like when you lift a fish from water, then lay it back on the surface, open your hands and it slips into the stream and swims away. He had slipped back, gently, to that current.

Very much like peeling the skin of an onion several things slipped off me without any words. One was the fear of death. I hadn't even known, before that, that I was afraid of death so much. But it peeled off me and was gone. A fish slips back into the water easily. Nothing to fear.

Another peel was the belief that nothing could happen to *me*. I was sitting stark and revealed on the hill with the suspended snow. Things could happen to me. It wasn't a scary thought, but more a blending with the way water runs down hill. Things could happen to me. There was no immunity, no protection.

I sat on the hill.

Chapter Sixteen

Keep on Walking

I have no idea how long I sat on the hill, or what possessed me to move. In a way, I've never moved off that hill. I'm sitting there still, with my dead baby inside the cabin, wrapped in his blankets, tiny dry snowflakes suspended in front of my eyes.

Some heartbreaks come upon us slowly. Some come with a flash. Modern wisdom says, just give yourself time and you will get over it. My experience tells me that it is better to keep these things as part of our souls. Heartbreak stays. There is no getting over it, and there shouldn't be. When the skin has peeled off, uncovering that stark nakedness underneath, there is nothing to do but stand there revealed. Heartbreak can tuck softly into the soul. There are places within you for these things to abide.

More and more, the wildness of the world outside was becoming the wildness of the world inside of me. A billion possibilities without, a billion possibilities within. My heart held a piece of winter now, like the snow tucked silently under the cliffs. Within the span of a moment it had made itself a permanent home.

Consolation was useless. People get upset when I tell them I know my baby's death was my fault. But I know that I was the one that didn't sleep with him that night—maybe he was too cold. I was the one who put the extra blanket on him—maybe he suffocated in all those blankets. I was the one who let him cry for the longest time. Maybe, I don't know…I didn't do it on purpose. All the same, I did do something wrong. It takes fault to a whole new level. Sometimes we do things with good intentions and still screw up. Sometimes we do our best and it comes out badly. Sometimes we do things with a conscious bad intention and it comes out okay. Inshallah. It is God's will. These things leave a vast space within us where holiness can live. We are not above it, we are not below it. We are it.

I had not read the manual this far. I had no idea what to do, but I knew that something had to be done. We probably needed to report what had happened. There was sure to be an authority or something for this sort of thing.

I knew we should go to town. I refused to pick up Jesse, so John did it. He wrapped the little bundle in blankets and placed it in the back of the station wagon. John drove us to Leadville. We stopped at the pay phone by the Safeway store. Inside the icy booth I slipped a dime into the slot and dialed the Sheriff's office. I held the phone steady as a man answered; I asked him what we should do. Unfortunately it happened to be Sunday. In a small town in the mountains of Colorado nobody works on Sunday.

I wanted an autopsy because I wanted to know if I had suffocated my baby. I had this strange suspicion that that's what had happened. John said that when he picked Jesse up his mouth had a little suction to the sheet. You can't get autopsies in Leadville on Sunday. The sheriff told us that we would have to drive to Denver and go to a hospital to request the autopsy. So we did. We drove, silently, into the traffic of Denver. We hadn't eaten. We didn't talk. We just drove, pulling into Denver near five o'clock; dusk was starting to take over the gray sky.

We went to the Community General Hospital because we heard they do things for poor people for free. We found a parking place and scraggled slowly into the emergency room; John was holding our little bundle. At the desk we told the people what had happened and asked if we could get an autopsy. They treated us like we were making an order at the drive in window; we filled out papers and they took Jesse.

Then we stood there and waited. Stocking caps still on our heads, dirty jeans and old coats.

A young doctor came back. We were getting some attention now because he questioned us critically; "The baby is awful cold, are you sure he didn't freeze to death?"

John answered, "Yes. We are sure. He was still warm when I picked him up."

I explained that we had driven for hours through the winter mountains with no heat in the back of the Volvo.

He took our word. Maybe it was because we looked so pathetic. They kept Jesse. Now the hospital was finished with us. There was nothing to do but wait two days for the autopsy; we turned around and drove back to Leadville. We stayed that night in Tim and Courtney's house. They were good friends. A short explanation was all they asked of us.

There are a lot of terrible logistics to deal with when you have a baby that dies. The next morning John and I walked over to the funeral home to tell them that the hospital would be sending Jesse and the autopsy up when the latter was done. Down on Main Street we saw Janet. She was a block away and started running towards us shouting, "Hey you guys! How's the baby?"

How are you supposed to answer that question? We ducked quickly up a side street and hurried off so she couldn't catch us.

Still Wondering

Jesse and the autopsy arrived at the funeral home on Tuesday. The autopsy report was very complicated and there was no one to explain it to us. I tried to read it. It seemed to indicate that he had died from pneumonia. I wondered, "How could that be? Wouldn't he have been coughing or had a fever or something like that?" Getting the autopsy didn't answer any of my questions. It just made me feel worse.

It was several years until I first heard the term Sudden Infant Death Syndrome, or SIDS. I felt I had suffocated Jesse in his crib with too many blankets. Can babies die for no reason? That's what the theory of Sudden Infant Death seemed to indicate.

Around 1995 doctors began to suspect that Sudden Infant Death Syndrome can be caused by putting babies on their stomachs to sleep, especially if they are lying on a soft bed and have too many blankets on them. Their new lungs can't breathe in enough oxygen. Sometimes they build up a little pocket of carbon dioxide in the blankets near their mouth and run out of air while they are sleeping.

When I heard that, I felt immediately that this was the answer I had always known—putting him on his stomach, and putting on that extra blanket to keep him warm—that was the thing. Nowadays common wisdom says to put a baby to sleep on its back.

We had to stop at the health clinic in town for some final paperwork. And there was Janet. She pounced on us with determination. She was practically in tears, confronting us and demanding to know why we didn't like her any more—after all she'd done for us. I tried to explain, "Listen, the thing is that the baby is dead and we really don't want everyone walking up to us and asking, "How's the baby?"

I decided she could be of some use. I gave her instructions to go to every single person in Leadville that might possibly know us and tell them what had happened so that nobody else would walk up to me and say, "How's the baby?"

One of the strange things about having a baby that dies is what to do with all the baby stuff. I had a little tub for him to bathe in and some clothes. I knew a few girls who were pregnant and I tried to give the stuff away. Nobody wants stuff from a dead baby. Like it might be catching or something. I finally brought it all over to the Goodwill and left it there.

Another Winter

John and I went back to the cabin.

Even though my life had completely changed, it was also right back to what it had been before. I needed something different. And then a stroke of luck. Courtney had a new girlfriend named Nan. She had a job at the Ski Cooper Ski Area on Tennessee Pass managing the lunch counter. Tennessee Pass was halfway between Homestake Creek and Leadville. Nan hired me as her assistant. Perfect. The ski area was only opened on the weekends. I could handle that.

Now I had a schedule. I would get up from Homestake Creek early Saturday morning and ski out. I had to go whether it was blizzard, sunny, cold, freezing…it didn't matter. For me this was perfect; a ski trip can happen in any weather.

At the highway I would stash my skis in the bushes and hitchhike to the ski area. Almost every time the first car would pick me up. I think they were curious why some gal would be standing out in a snowstorm on a remote mountain highway. I would hop out at the top of the mountain and be ready for work.

All day I made sandwiches and served food to the skiers. At night I'd ride with Nan back down to Leadville. Then I'd spend the night sleeping on the floor. Sunday morning it was back up to the ski area, and I'd work all day again. At the end of the day, dusk coming on, I would hitchhike back down to Homestake Creek and ski out to the cabin.

Early Saturday morning I would strap my skis to my boots and kick-slide down the driveway in the first light of dawn before the sun had managed to climb over the eastern mountains. As I skied I could see the sunlight edge down the eastward slopes to my left. To my right was the creek gurgling under its icepack and upward, the backside of the peaks of the Continental Divide. Surrounding me was a deep, omnipresent cold that touched any piece of bare skin like a sharp hand. I could feel this sharpness as the cold air touched my lungs with each inhalation. The thin, high-altitude air held 20 degrees below zero in its everyday vocabulary.

Clear days were bright and cold. Stormy days were warmer. I would ski through a world where whiteness was everything—below me, above me, and all around me, sweating under my coat. White stuff gathered on my shoulders and stocking cap. It turned the trail in front of me invisible. As I floated forward, all I could see was a triangular wake of snow slicing away from the curved tips of my skis.

It's hard to say if I liked it best when it was sunny or when it was snowing. Snow kept me warm and safe, but there was nothing to see. The cold turned the world into a shining paradise of glitter, but this cold can bite the lungs, freezing those small bronchia that bring oxygen to the blood.

I always wrapped a scarf around my face and pulled a thick hat over my ears. Long underwear and wool socks were an everyday thing. Heading out of my cabin on my skis, I was a bundle of clothes, with glasses sticking through the crack between scarf and hat.

On cold days, the laws of physics caused me grief. Breath is wet stuff. When warm wet air hits frozen dry air the moisture turns into steam and rises. My wet breath would slip up the crack, under my scarf, each side of my nose, just below my eyes, shooting an icy fog under the lenses of my glasses. This fog froze in front of my vision in ever-thickening layers. I tried pinching the scarf around my nose to force the wet breath straight out through the weave of the scarf. No good. Every exhale put another layer of ice over my vision.

There was nothing to do but take the glasses off, stick them down inside my coat, in a pocket near my chest to warm. Then the world was a bright blur. I could keep going okay, but I craved to see the beauty around me. I knew that I needed to keep the scarf over my nose, but I also needed to see. Finally I'd give in. I'd stop my forward motion, pull the warmed glasses from my pocket, put them back on my nose, and tuck the scarf down below my mouth so it only covered my chin. Lung capillaries sustained permanent damage.

The four-mile ski trips turned my disaster into peace. I had snow, freedom, a little money, and activity. If I had been living in a house in town commuting to a job in a car, it would have had no therapeutic value. As it was, I was forced to ski in and out once a week, through the mountainous world of Homestake Creek valley. This trip was a beautiful snow-filled, crystal paradise that brought me back to myself.

Truck

John went into town a few times during the winter, working odd jobs and the like. The Volvo was sitting in the garage, snowed in with us. In the early spring John got tired of hitching rides and drove his old truck out to the beginning of the Homestake Creek road. He parked far into the plowed turnoff to protect it from snowplows.

Then one day, we skied out and there was the truck, with the beautiful windshield smashed in. Maybe a rock from a snowplow had hit it, but I doubt it, because the truck was parked way off to the side. It looked like someone had come up with a sledgehammer and given the windshield one big smack.

It was the last straw. Colorado didn't want us any more, and we didn't want Colorado. This place had become too crowded. Bad things happen here. We wanted to go find a real wilderness.

We were also worried about Ray Kelley because his asthma was getting worse. We thought he should get out of the high altitude, to someplace with more air and more sun. As soon as we were able to get out in the spring John, Sheela, and I said temporary goodbyes to Ray, as well as Stubby and the other cats. We packed the Volvo with supplies and cooking gear and headed north. We headed back up to Idaho to hike and then to Washington to the apple orchards. We were looking for another home. Our intention was to find some place with a lower altitude, and yet, out in the woods; a place that Ray would really like. Maybe that would make him better.

My boots weren't new any more. They'd been through snow and mud and desert. The inside fronts under the ball were worn down smooth from many miles; the tread was gone. They weren't so reliable now and slipped out from under me at the worst moments. Moisture seeped in through the thin leather. My life was slipping on towards something new.

We'll speed through the next eight years of this story because I was now more involved in being what I had become, than in becoming what I wanted to be.

We found that there were lots of jobs in apple orchards besides picking apples. We looked for orchard jobs near Boise, traveled through Salmon, Idaho, and backpacked down into the canyons of the Middlefork of the Salmon River. I was pregnant again in July. Once more my life was coming full circle. I hiked through the mountains with my growing belly. By late summer we were looking for an orchard that was hiring in Chellan, Washington.

We picked the whole season and then found some people who had a house they wanted us to caretake while they took off for the winter. We rented that house, paid our money, got in the car and drove to Leadville to get our stuff.

We drove out to Homestake Creek and told Ray what was going on. This was a good place and we were ready to go. He wasn't quite in the mood to pack up and go right that minute, so we told him that we would be back the next summer for him. By then we would have the perfect place.

We drove long days, heading back north. On the second night we stopped in Salmon, Idaho and rented a hotel room. It was getting pretty cold for camping, and it was also the day before Thanksgiving. The hotel was off Main Street in the Old Herndon Building. It had a row of rooms upstairs with a shared bathroom down the hall. Our window was at the end, facing west. Rent was pretty cheap so we decided to stay a few days and check out the town.

As we were heading out for breakfast the next morning, the girl at the front desk told us that the downstairs door to the hotel was going to be locked that day. It was Thanksgiving. Everybody in Salmon took Thanksgiving off so they could have dinner with their families. We had a choice: we could be locked in or locked out until the manager came back that evening.

The decision was obvious, we did not want to be locked inside! We grabbed a few things and went out. It took about ten minutes for us to get tired of walking up and down the Main Street in Salmon, so we decided to drive up to Hamilton, Montana, to see if we might like it there.

John was starting to think he liked Idaho better than Washington, because it was more remote. I liked Hamilton a lot better than Salmon because it looked more innovative. We got in the Volvo and drove out of town. Just before the little town of North Fork we hit a rock in the middle of the highway. Its sharp upper point busted a hole in the gas tank. I watched as the gas gauge needle fell towards the "E" and all the gas leaked out.

So there we were, stuck in North Fork, Idaho. Nobody was working. Nobody was doing anything. We sat by the side of the road for about an hour and finally managed to catch a ride back to Salmon.

Now what? We wandered up and down the streets of Salmon. Nothing was open, we couldn't get into our hotel, and our car was broken down 20 miles out on the highway.

After awhile we noticed there were lots of people going in and out of the Lantern Bar. We went in and it turned out they are having a Thanksgiving feast for all the people who didn't have families in town. It was all free, potatoes, sweet potatoes, salad, pumpkin pie—everything you could imagine. The people were friendly. They welcomed us in, listened to our story, and filled our table with food. We were the first vegetarians they had ever met and I think they were curious to see how many vegetables we could eat.

It was the old-timer drunk Salmon crowd. We fit right in. There I was, five months pregnant, our car was broken down, we were locked out of our hotel room until that evening, and we got fed the best Thanksgiving a person could ever hope for. We decided to live in Salmon, Idaho. A broken vehicle had sent us away from Colorado, and now a broken car landed us in Salmon.

The next day we got the car towed into town. John bought a patch and figured out how to put it on the gas tank so that it would hold gas. We found a little cabin for sale for three thousand dollars. It turned out that John had a friend in Leadville who was a trust fund kid. This guy liked to give friends money, or something like that. I never really quite understood exactly how the transaction happened. But he gave John three thousand dollars and we bought the cabin.

Imagine that. There we were buying, *buying*, a home in this small town for three thousand dollars. So now, here we were. Living in this little cabin that was hardly more than a shack in the town of Salmon, Idaho. We had electricity in there, and there was a hot water heater and a toilet—a flush toilet—and a bathtub. This was a big luxury for us; we had really come up in the world.

The cabin had a tarpaper roof. It was heated with a full-size, green cookstove. This was very much the same lifestyle we had been living, only we were in town and we had electricity.

John left me in Salmon and drove up to Washington to get the stuff that we had left at the house and to tell the people that we wouldn't be caretaking for them after all. When he came back, we fixed up the cabin as best we could. Not as best we *could*, but as best we could using no materials and spending no money.

We had no jobs. I was six months pregnant by then. We didn't know any people in town. But there we were.

To this day when people ask me how I came to live in Salmon, I tell them, "That's where the car broke down."

Chapter Seventeen

Flash Forward

Ray Kelley died that winter. Fishback skied out for one of his visits and found him in his cabin; it was another failure for me. My life was developing holes all over it. We should have never let him stay out that winter by himself. He hadn't been by himself for three winters. It was too much. That wasn't the only way we failed him; the next summer the Forest Service came and bulldozed the cabins. Ray Kelley's dreams, hopes, and creativity were all gone. Tim managed to remove one of the cabins before it was bulldozed, but the cats disappeared into the wilderness and were never taken care of again. The two things that Ray was terrified would happen had happened.

My life was starting to collect a 'mistakes' packet. A list of should-have-dones and could-have-done-betters. One of the reasons for religion in human beings, I think, is to deal with the fact that we are not always right. The more we try to be right, the more we become wrong. The things collecting in my packet were the sorts of things people search for redemption from. I didn't have time to worry about it too much. I was being pulled forward by the events in my real-time life.

We found a midwife in Salmon and I had the baby in March: Jaimos. We gave him a middle name after Tim's invisible friend. So he was Jaimos Franklin Skriletz. We called him Jaime. The only problem with this birth was that I had the baby so fast we weren't able to get the midwife there in time, so John delivered Jaimos. Annette, the midwife in Salmon, was out of her house for the afternoon and got the message that I was in labor after I had delivered. Oh well.

Jaime was healthy. This time, instead of reading books about how to take care of a baby, I watched Sheela. She had a litter of puppies at the same time. She would feed them whenever they yapped and bite them if they annoyed her. I never bit Jaime, but I was more relaxed in taking care of him.

I dug a garden as the sun started warming the ground. We were in the lowlands now and I was determined to grow something. I got myself back in shape chopping at the rocky mountain dirt with my pick.

John got a job with the Forest Service, on the Trail Crew. This suited him pretty well because he could spend the whole summer traveling around the different trails of the Salmon National Forest. He was on the Cobalt district working on the trails in the wilderness area. Most of the time he was away from the office and out on the trails, cutting brush and shoveling landslides so that people would be able to go hiking out there.

During his travels he asked around and found this deserted piece of property on Beaver Creek, which is a tributary of Panther Creek, seven miles from where it joins the Salmon River. A rich guy from California had bought the place nine years ago and it had been sitting empty ever since. Packrats moved into the house and vandals broke the windows. It was 60 miles into the wilderness from Salmon, which was 180 miles away from anywhere to start with. There was a big orchard there, slowly dying from neglect, and we were experienced with orchard work. They gave us permission to move in as the first snows of winter were flying.

We lived out there for seven years.

We had two more babies: girls. I had each baby in Salmon, but not at the hospital. I think my relationship with my midwife, Annette, was jinxed, because she didn't make it to Tessa's birth either. The poor midwife actually had to be rushed to the hospital with appendicitis! But for Kacey, our youngest girl, she made it and it was really a treat to be taken care of while in labor. I had my blood pressure taken, and all sorts of other medical stuff. I felt very safe. This was a good thing too, since Kacey was over nine pounds and a bit a of job to deliver. I needed the extra encouragement that Annette provided. A couple days after each birth we all headed back to our wilderness home.

Beaver Creek had a huge orchard. We mowed, pruned, and thinned. We got the irrigation going, watered the trees, put windows into the house, and fixed up the property.

The road up to our new home was only two miles from the plowed road, but a good three-hour drive from the closest town. We were never snowed in more than three months each winter. Unfortunately, we were also in a deep canyon and didn't get any sun on our house for two and a half months! I felt like a mole.

I grew huge gardens out there. This was real self-sufficiency and was supposed to be great (in my mind). Once again I was learning that if you put yourself in an extreme situation you learn things about reality that otherwise remain hidden. You can't do it all yourself! Part of being a natural human was having a tribe and community about you to share the workload. I seemed to be all by myself at Beaver Creek. The harder I worked, the more work I created for myself.

My gardens grew larger each year. I wanted to be self-sufficient, but the work was overwhelming. With all the plowing and planting and weeding, by the time it came to canning I was exhausted. I remember one day going out to the garden to pick cucumbers for pickles. The only way to keep a cucumber patch thriving is to pick the cucumbers each day. I was hoping to keep up with volume by not letting the cucs get too big. My plan didn't work. The more I picked the more the little cucumbers grew. On this day, I went out and filled three five-gallon buckets with baby cucumbers. I fell down in the dirt and wept, hugging the last bucket—it still needed to be washed, pickled, and canned. It was too much. Growing enough food for a village is the job of a village.

I grew almost all our food. I canned everything. After Tessa was born we realized we needed meat in our diets and gave up on being vegetarians.

Still, we wanted to be natural do-it-yourselfers. It only seemed right that we would also do our own butchering. We got some chickens, and we got milk goats so I would have plenty of milk for the kids.

To get our milk goats to give milk, they first had to have babies. To get goats to have babies you have to get a billy goat. Living way out in the woods there was no easy way to take our goats somewhere for servicing. But it turned out that my midwife in town had a billy goat we could use. Annette gave us the billy goat for free with one condition—we were never to bring him back. This speaks volumes about billy goats.

This was the smelliest, dumbest animal I had ever encountered. He was quite pleased to take care of the needs of our two pretty little Nubian goats. So pleased, in fact, that he peed all over himself to make sure he was of the right attractive stench for the girls. He peed, and smiled his horny billy goat smile, tongue panting from the side of his mouth, and found every opportunity to rub his smelly side across my leg.

After we were certain that the billy had done his job, we were faced with a strange dilemma. There was no way we were going to let him live with us through the winter, but there was no place to take him. We were faced with our first butchering opportunity. We didn't think that we would want to eat a whole billy goat. It was bound to be tough and terrible tasting, but we were determined to eat some of him and were determined to butcher him properly.

John did the evil deed. He tied the goat to a tree, shot him and slit his throat so all the blood would drain out. We wanted to hang the body head down to let the blood drain free, so John tied a rope to his hind legs and slung the rope up over the branch of a tree.

I couldn't believe how heavy he was as we pulled the rope over the branch. My strength wasn't equal to John's, so we couldn't get him all the way up. I leaned back on the rope to keep him lifted off the ground and John cut off his head to lighten the load. Then we were able to get the body up off the ground and draining. Once the carcass was hanging in the tree John and I worked together to cut and peel his smelly, urine-stained skin off and put it in a solution to soak for tanning later. I hauled the head off into the woods to dispose of it. We cleaned up from our gory task, ate dinner, put the kids to bed and went to sleep.

The next morning I got up, walked into the living room, looked out the window and there, staring in at me, was the billy goat's head leering its tongue-dripping billy-goat grin. The head was propped on the lawn, perfectly arranged, facing my window, staring right at me.

Sheela had found the head and brought it back to the yard to chew on. I dragged it *far* out in the woods this time.

During these years I learned about animals being food. I was starting to have a sneaking suspicion that I was also food.

I learned about quail and how part of being quail was being food for other things. Quails were amazing creatures to live with. In the spring, all on one day it seems, mama quails and baby quails appear everywhere. Each mama has about twelve babies. Everywhere you go you see mama quail and twelve little babies rushing and bumping behind. By the end of the summer you are down to individual quails again.

Summer after summer I watched mama with her string of babies. The first day she has twelve. The next day it's ten. A week later they are getting bigger and now five are following. A few weeks later they are almost full-grown and there are three. Finally in summer you see the mama quail and one baby quail almost her size; that's the one that survived. At the end of the summer there are only individual quails again—just about the same number that started in the spring. Most of the baby quails were food for something else.

One day, late in the fall, when the garden was black and wrinkled from the first frosts, I was out pulling up vines from the dirt. A big old fat quail came walking into the garden. She poked her beak around in the dirt, ignoring me. It was probably one of the baby quails that I had watched first in large groups, then smaller groups as it grew up. It seemed determined to become my food.

John had been having fun hunting quails with his twenty-two rifle. I also had a hunting license that year in case I ever got the time to get out and do some hunting. But, there was the quail, pecking in the garden as if I weren't there. I thought it would make a pretty good dinner. So I picked up a stick, walked quietly over to the quail with it looking right at me and hit at it with my stick.

It was a perfect clean miss. The bird just stood there looking at me. I stood looking at it. What was this about? The hunter *never* gets a second chance! I picked up the stick again, recalculated my aim and whap! Hit it clean on the head. Quail for dinner. I wonder how many chances it would have given me.

I never turned into a great hunter. There were two main reasons. One was that I never had a babysitter for the kids and couldn't get out, but mainly, I did not like carrying the heavy gun through the woods. My desire to kill something for dinner was not greater than my dislike of carrying a long heavy metal stick.

I do have one good hunting story though. I had a friend named Sheila. It was a little strange when I would yell for my dog, because she would think I was yelling at her, but she was a good friend and lived up in Cobalt, a half hour drive up Panther Creek. She was married to a guy named Clark. Clark and John would often go hunting together, and Sheila was a good hunter too. Sheila was better at spotting animals out in the woods than anyone I've ever met.

One time, when they were visiting us, Sheila and I told the guys that it wasn't fair that I didn't get to go hunting, so we left the guys home with the kids and Sheila and I set out on the hunt. We hiked two miles up Beaver Creek road and then headed up a steep ridge. Sheila amazed me by pointing out three does resting behind a log. I could hardly see them, even with Sheila pointing them out to me. Finally one wagged her ear and my eye caught the movement. I learned on that day that there are millions of things around me that I never even see.

We headed up a north-facing ridge in search of a buck. The mountains out of Beaver Creek are steep and rocky. We climbed silently, following a fairly fresh trail. The ridge we were on jutted up steeply from the creek bottom. Sheila drifted towards the left side of the ridge as she climbed, and I drifted to the right until we were out of sight of each other. It was no problem; we knew we could see more territory this way and we both knew where we were going, so we weren't lost.

I was hiking along my side of the ridge when all of the sudden I heard the rattle of hooves and falling rocks above me. I looked up and there were three giant big horn rams leaping off the cliff at me. They were coming at full speed! One had a full curl to his horns, and the other two were at least a half curl. These were old experienced rams, plunging at me from above.

I jumped and stood up straight. They caught my sudden movement and veered off to the side, leaping from the rocks and charging over the ridge top. I caught my breath and hurried over the ridge to find Sheila and tell her what I had seen. I found her sitting, ashen face, on the ground. Those three rams had charged over the ridge straight at her. She escaped by falling quickly to the side. She had come within inches of being trampled by Rocky Mountain Sheep!

We figured that some hunters up the hill had spooked the rams down on us. They were running fast and straight. We didn't have permits to shoot sheep, but had fun making up the story we could have told if we *had* shot them.

"No officer, we aren't poachers. It was self defense! We can prove it! Look—the bullet hole goes *up* into the belly. We shot them as they were jumping over us!"

That's a good hunting story, even though we didn't get anything that day. It was us who had become the hunted!

Town

Eventually, it was time for Jaime to go to school. John and I were having problems. John would hang out in the winter and collect unemployment checks. In the summer he worked trail crew on the Forest Service, which he was increasingly growing to hate every year. I was trying to make money with a little business selling handspun yarn and knitted items.

The trail crew schedule had John working ten days on and then four days off. Sometimes he would go to work for ten days, then off on a backpacking trip for four days and then back to work ten more days in the wilderness area. Sometimes he would do that twice. This would leave me home at Beaver Creek all by myself with three kids (starting with one, then two, then three kids) for weeks in a row. I was washing fleeces, pruning the orchard, growing gardens, canning food, raising babies, and baking bread. I often went months without seeing an adult human being.

The problem was that when John came home he wouldn't help. He figured that he was off working the job and I was home doing nothing. So he wouldn't help much in the garden. He wouldn't help much with the kids. And he was drinking more and more. I was getting pretty grouchy about the whole thing.

John lived in a culture of beer. Every event called for a beer. When they went on their 10-day trail crew trips they took one whole mule just to carry the beer. Off work, when we visited friends, it was an opportunity to get drunk.

My original intention had been to homestudy all the kids. My goal was to raise perfect, angelic kids that were unpolluted by modern American society. I wanted to make sure that the kids were ahead of their class, so I was already teaching Jaime how to read and count. He didn't go to kindergarten, but he was already working on second grade material.

It was time for Jaime to start first grade. I already had a taste of the amount of work home schooling was going to be. It was going to add a lot to my already heavy workload. So, one day I asked John, "Are you going to do your half of the home schooling?"

He looked at me with a puzzled expression and said, "What do you mean? That's not my job. That's your job."

I looked back and said, "I'm not going to do my *HALF* either."

I packed up the kids and moved into town, back into our little cabin.

I knew that was going to be the end of us. I didn't think John was going to able to handle living in town, because he didn't want to live in town. But, for me, something had to change.

After two weeks, John gave up and decided to move in too. That left us really crowded in the cabin. Shortly after, we bought an old house down the street. We paid fifteen thousand dollars.

John's mother helped us with the down payment. But now we had house payments, electric bills, and a phone. We had a water bill. Can you believe that they actually charge for water *and* sewer? Every month. You have to pay for the water to come into your house, and also for it to go back out again! Quite a surprise for me!

There I was, living in town. All those years of avoiding it, and suddenly I was in it. I was as lost as a city guy on a wilderness camping trip. Everything about it made me feel tense. How do I pay for all this stuff? Month after month the bills flowed toward me like a raging river.

The marriage didn't last too long after that. John had too much access to beer now. He spent his time down at the Owl Club drinking. My friends told me I needed to go to an Alanon meeting.

Alanon is this group of people who are the spouses of alcoholics. So I went to a few meetings. The first time there were quite a few people there. They talked about their lives, saying, "Oh my drunk husband did this, and oh my drunk husband did that. And I'm trying to feel good about myself and I'm trying to deal with it." Everyone had long stories. We said little prayers and went home.

When I went to the second meeting the same people were there. One particular older lady had a long story that night. She said, "Oh my husband did this, and oh he did that. And I'm trying to deal with it, and I'm trying to feel good about myself." We read little prayers about how we should learn to feel good about ourselves.

I had a growing sense of unease. Finally I asked this older gal, "How long has your husband been a drunk?"

She said, "Forty years."

I asked her, "How long have you been coming to Alanon?"

She replied, "Twenty years."

And I thought, *yikes! You mean this is my future!* On and on, never-ending, dealing with John's drunkenness. I freaked out, went home and threw John out of the house.

He went back East for awhile. His brother gave him a job building a house in Connecticut. I was hoping it would sober him up a little bit. It was awfully hard on John, I'll admit. But life improved immediately for me and the kids.

Even though we were never officially married, we did have to get officially divorced. I paid for the lawyer by typing a large manual full of legal forms. I couldn't afford to pay for a babysitter, and the lawyer didn't have an extra computer for me to type on during the day. So I would get up at 3:00 a.m., make myself a big thermos of coffee, drive down to the lawyer's office, let myself in with a key and type for three hours. My kids slept soundly in the mornings and were always still asleep when I tip-toed back into the house before seven o'clock. At that time I would get them up, get Jaimos off to the school bus, and pack the two girls over to the daycare where I had managed to get a job.

I learned how to use a computer that winter even though I had to give up on sleep entirely. I kept myself going day after day by not having time to think about it.

Chapter Eighteen

Living Native in America

We were so poor that when I compared my income to poverty level statistics in the United States, I wasn't even on the chart for a family of four.

Once again, I was faced with the challenge of becoming. Becoming a new person in human society. Only now I didn't have a Ray Kelley to lead me through the wilderness ahead. It was like I had been taken out of a movie in which I knew and understood the script and thrown into a foreign film. I had lived so many years out in the woods, where I understood how things worked. All the sudden I was dealing with a world that had been created by people that I didn't understand.

In many ways I was like a person from centuries ago who had suddenly been transported in time into the twentieth century. I wasn't acclimatized to movies; TV sucked me into its vortex. I wasn't used to paying electric bills, phone bills. The time machine had dumped me into a very strange place.

At the same time I was surrounded by the most opulent life I could imagine. I had this knob on my sink that I could turn and hot water came out!! The same knob was on my bathtub. I could sit in there, turn it on and splash around in hot water! I could wash my hair without using a bucket. Electric lights are amazing. Flick. And there they are. No matches, no gas fumes, no nothing. Just great light. Nobody else seems to notice.

To this day, I am amazed at the way people live. Everything is backward. Riches have made us poor. Everyone is surrounded by total opulent luxury and yet there is nothing but stress. Bills pile up; we don't know what to do.

I have machines that do jobs all by themselves that used to take me hours. Like my washing machine. I put soap in it, put clothes in it, shut the lid, turn it on, and go away. It washes, rinses and spins my clothes until they are clean.

I have mixers that mix things. I have a microwave oven. Yet people complain and complain. We have so much and nobody is satisfied.

We live in almost perfect safety. Yes, there's crime, but watch the news and look at what is happening to other people. There are no wars in our backyard. There are all these people. Look at how many people there are and how closely we are packed together and be amazed at how peacefully we are really living together.

I can walk down the street and 99% of the people I meet are going to be kind and gracious to me. That's a miracle, and it is because most of the people have their basic needs met. We live in luxury and it makes us easy.

Water runs into our homes. Toilets flush away our waste, and simply take it away. Flush, that's all. You never even see it. Somebody else takes care of it.

Our cars are amazing. They just go. We have beautiful roads to drive on. Electricity surges into our homes. You can flick on a switch and the lights come on. Bright lights too. You don't have to squint and try to see. You can sit there and just read. You can sit there and just knit, with the lights on. You can see what you are doing.

Our discontent leads to our greed. We are richer than any King of old. It is total opulence. And people complain. They complain about paying taxes. Like the government is doing something against us. We make more money in a day than a person in a third world country makes in a year, and yet complain about giving a bit of it away to taxes. Look around at the absolute luxury that we live in—that these taxes give us. If something happens we can call the police, and they come. If our house catches on fire the firemen come. If someone is sick they can go to the hospital and it's there.

There are people who have dedicated their whole lives just to be ready so that if you get sick you have someplace to go. We have universities!!! People can go there and just learn stuff. We don't have to make everything up from scratch.

Statistically I am right there with the poorest people in our society. And yet I have so much. There are services for our every need. We have schools with whole teams of people just to teach children. The school system is far from perfect, but what a blessing to be able to send kids off to a place that is completely dedicated to nothing but teaching. We don't have to do everything by ourselves. Believe me, I know what a blessing this is.

Still the Problems

But back to my immediate problems. Becoming a natural human being cannot be considered a career choice in the twentieth century. This was something that I did to myself, and not something that anyone did to me. Part of being a natural human was becoming a good mother, and that turned out to not be a paying position. It's no mystery to me why we have so many mean kids with attitude in our world. It's because mothers are not honored.

I was struggling with an impossible situation. I could get a job for minimum wage, which was four dollars an hour at the time, and then pay a dollar an hour, per child for childcare. That left me with a dollar an hour to live on: to make house payments, buy food, and pay any bills. I was overwhelmed with a gray weight of helplessness and the hopelessness of poverty.

Living out in the woods, it hadn't mattered. I could make the things I wanted. But making things takes time. Now I had a poverty of everything. I didn't have any money to buy things, and I didn't have the time to make or grow the things I needed.

I had traded one impossible do-it-yourself situation for another impossible do-it-yourself situation. There were lots of people in town, and lots of luxuries, but nobody to help out. The idea that one little mother can do all the things that are needed to take care of small ones is insane.

Living out in the woods, the attitude of paying attention to the weather and air was compatible to paying attention to children, because children are a part of the wind and air. In town, paying attention to money cannot be done in the presence of the children. It has to be done off someplace at work, a place where children are nothing more than a disturbance.

To this day I still can't figure out how to do it. I've tried working jobs and find that I always have to say, "No, be quiet, sit down," to the children. I've tried working at home and find that I don't make much money and always have to say, "Don't bother me now," to the children.

I've been a big failure in making money. But I think I've done okay with the children. They've grown into wonderful people and they don't seem to be too mad at me. So this is what I have to say: natural people honor children and mothers. They also honor the responsibility and beauty of being a father.

I think natural people must laugh a lot. They don't have too much to do. They have lots of other relaxed people to joke with. All we have to do to have a wonderful world to live in is to remember what it is like to be a true human being. Then we'll go back to wanting simplicity.

Chapter Nineteen

The Environmentalist and the Fox

Being very poor in a society in which most people know how to make money has been a strange situation—especially for a person like me, who has the psychological disadvantage of thinking she is rich.

I have always been interested in preserving the environment. So I joined an environmental group called the Idaho Conservation League. I first got involved with the group while living at Beaver Creek. One year was very cold and ice jams in the river clogged up the water and flooded property from North Fork all the way up river to Salmon. The residents were upset at getting flooded and demanded that the government "fix" the river. I thought the idea of "fixing" a river (which had been flowing through the valley for millenniums before white people came along) was silly.

One thing I had learned in irrigating the orchard was that water flowed where it wished. My mind could try to figure out which direction was downhill, but the water just *went* downhill, no thought, just the never-ending force of gravity. This was the same with the river. It was going to go where it wanted to go. "Fixing" it would have done nothing but make it ugly.

I was interested in becoming a writer and was asked to work up some articles about the river. I had a wonderful time researching the problem, composing the articles, typing up finished manuscripts on my two-dollar, second-hand Royal typewriter, and seeing my name in print in the publications.

The gal who ran the Idaho Conversation League in Salmon was named Lil. Now that I was living in town she thought it would be a great idea if I went to a meeting of the members of the League, which was to be held in Stanley at a cross-country ski lodge. I was hesitant about going. We argued. I explained that I didn't have any money to pay for lodging and food. She said the League would pay for my attendance. Dinner cost five dollars—surely I had five dollars. My pride wouldn't let me admit that I didn't really have five dollars.

She said she'd drive me. All I had to do was find someone to babysit the kids. Lil insisted that I would love meeting the people, and I would love the resort because she knew I'd done a lot of cross-country skiing. She finally convinced me to go by telling me that the Cross Country Ski Lodge served the best food.

"It worth going just for the food." she said.

So I agreed. Since we had moved to town I had eaten nothing but homemade soup and homemade bread, day after day, because that was all I could afford. I was dying for a good meal.

I found a babysitter and rode with Lil to the meeting of the Idaho Conservation League.

I never felt so out of place in my whole life. Here were all these young professional people; doctors, lawyers, people with jobs, people with careers, people who were interested in preserving the wilderness but had never done more than visit the wilderness, as if it were a museum, or a pretty zoo. These people felt as comfortable in society as I felt in a snow-filled canyon. I felt as comfortable with them as a trapped raccoon. To me they were the same perplexing creatures as the ones I met at the Colorado Mountain Club at Homestake Creek. I couldn't think of a thing to say to anyone. I hovered silently in the corner of the lodge.

The ski lodge was strange to me. People would pay to come to this place so they could go cross-country skiing on the trails. I couldn't understand it. To me skiing was a tool to get someplace or a way to see a really wild mountain. Here people paid to do it. They skied on groomed trails that went around a meadow. A circle around the meadow, that's all.

My teeth clenched of their own accord as I hovered in my corner. My poverty was wearing me like a cloak. All these people had safety and security and leisure to ski for fun; I had nothing but knowing how to breathe and listen with my elbows and three unkempt children waiting for me at home.

Finally it was time to eat, and my stomach was roaring. I was hungry for this wonderful food from the lodge. This was the one reason I had come, the only thing I could hang on to. We all filed into the dining room and sat down politely at a wooden table. It had been a long time since I had eaten in company, particularly with company such as this. I sat with anticipation, trying to remember how to be polite at a table, and waited for the food to come. My blood sugar had hit rock bottom, so my hands were trembling slightly.

Out walked the waitresses and they put big pots of homemade soup and trays of homemade bread on the long wooden table. I'm still waiting for the good food. The saliva in my mouth doesn't know where to go. I ask Lil, "Is this it, or is this just the beginning of the real food?"

She's scarfing down her soup with a big smile. "Isn't it great? Isn't this the best?"

Tears welled to my eyes and my poor little stomach clenched tight as I filled my wooden bowl with soup and took a piece of crusty bread. What sort of a world was I in?

I handed over my five dollars, feeling no weight in my hands.

The Environmentalists and the Fox

Lil managed to drag me out to one more environmentalist meeting with the Idaho Conservation League. I resisted going to this meeting too, but she convinced me that it would be a good career move. Since I had never made a career move in my life I figured it was probably about time to make one.

In my quest to be a writer one of the techniques I found useful was called clustering. It's a very simple idea. You put the idea you want to write about in a circle, then make lots of other circles around it and write in your ideas. It's a brainstorming technique that makes your ideas flow like the round circles. Suddenly you know what to say. It's most useful in capturing a good first sentence. It lets your brain focus on what is the most important quality in your thoughts.

Lil wanted me to give a workshop to all the members of the Idaho Conservation League on this clustering technique. The focus of this little workshop was how to start writing a letter to a Senator about an environmental issue. I agreed to go. I wasn't going to get paid, but I did get to go to the conference for free, and Lil drove me up.

We went to a big house on a ranch in Hailey, Idaho. I knew from the moment I saw the place that I was in trouble. This was a log *castle*. Huge. Big old-growth trees had been used to make the beams of the house. I was assured that these beams had come from already dead trees. The owners of the house had not been participating in deforesting the land. That didn't matter to me—I was shocked at the extravagance of the place and the amount of money it must have taken for the people to build it. It was far away from my world of poverty, tiny cabins, and mountain streams. And these were the people who were fighting *for* the environment.

The place made me uncomfortable. The knickknacks on the shelves were worth more than my yearly income. I didn't dare touch anything in this log castle or even breathe the air that was inside that house. I couldn't think of anything to talk about. They were all young professionals, and I was a single divorced mom who worked at a daycare center part time. I'd lived too long by myself; I didn't know any polite conversation for this situation. Somehow, I was supposed to be giving these people a talk about how to write a letter to their congressman.

I knew the trouble was rising for me when we were sitting on the couch after lunch. There were four of us. Everybody else was sitting in chairs. The conversation in the room was polite. I looked over and there was a spider crawling up the leg of the man sitting next to me.

He looks down, sees the spider and just sits there while the spider crawls up his leg. I guess the game immediately: killing or swiping the spider would not be a spiritual or environmental thing to do. His plan was to sit there and let the spider crawl across him and off in the direction of choice. Like moving it would throw it off its scent or something. My couchmate is obviously a pure guy, very spiritual.

I, on the other hand, watched with horror. The spider inched up his leg, heading towards me. I think, *"Oh, my God. What am I going to do?"* There was no way that I was going to let that spider crawl on me. I don't know anything about being spiritual or environmental, but I did know that no woodsman would let a spider crawl on her! It was instinct to brush the darn thing off.

If the spider showed up in any other situation I would fling it off me really quick, or smoosh it and then fling it off me. But, in this situation, I knew I couldn't do that. Conversation ground to a halt as the room of conference attendees watched. The spider slowly inched across the lap of this pure man heading towards me. I would look pretty bad if I squished it after all that.

Fortunately I was wise in the ways of spiders. I got a piece of paper off the coffee table and held it so that the spider crawled onto the piece of paper. Then I held the paper down near the ground and the spider crawled off into the house. The tension in the room dropped. We all remained pure and nothing got killed.

It was early afternoon now and things were going along okay. I wasn't cast from the group yet because I *had* let the spider live. All the same, I was not at ease.

There was one fellow that I actually got along with a little bit. He was a big, tall guy with a long beard. His name was Mitch. We had fun talking.

I told him where I had lived, and he seemed to like me. That afternoon I looked up from what I was doing and saw Mitch coming in through the full-glass double doors. He spotted me, came over and said, "Connie, do you know where I could find an axe?"

"What do you want an axe for?"

He said, "I found a fox just up the creek a little ways, and he's caught in a trap. I want to put him away." Just its hind leg had been caught, the leg was probably broken. The poor fox was trapped in misery, and there was no telling when the hunter, the trapper, would come check his traps. Mitch didn't like the idea of the fox suffering in the trap.

Mitch didn't dare tell any of the other people there about the fox because he knew it would turn into a horrible incident. I agreed with him on that, but I didn't have any idea where an axe could be found. We looked outside and we didn't find one. So Mitch went and asked the owner of the house. I watched as he told the story and saw the girl's eyes go wide.

She cried out, "There's a fox stuck in a trap up the creek."

As if they were one body, the environmentalists turned and rushed out the door to save the fox. I stood there in the living room in shock. I looked at Mitch, and he looked at me. "Oh my God, what is going to happen now?"

Together, Mitch and I followed behind the herd of environmentalists, who were rushing to save the fox. We were about ten paces behind. I looked up and there, walking down the creek from the other direction, was the hunter. This was going to be trouble.

The herd of environmentalists and the trapper arrived at the frightened fox at the same time. Mitch and I were about twenty seconds behind.

The poor trapper stood there in his plaid shirt and jeans, looking nonchalant and trying to be polite. The environmentalists were confronting him about his poor morals—how could he do such a terrible thing to the fox! The hunter explained that he has a permit, and that everything he was doing was legal. About that time I managed to catch up.

There was only one thing to do. I jumped in on the side of the hunter, trying to give him voice and calm things down. Better that the herd confronts me.

"Listen," I tell everyone. "This guy is completely within his rights; the laws are that he can trap this animal if he wants to. He's following the guidelines set by the Fish and Game. He has his permits; he's obviously a very good hunter because he's here checking his trap within a half-hour of the animal getting trapped in it. You have no quarrel with this man; he is in his rights."

The hunter looked at me, a little shocked, 'Whoa, where did she come from?'

The environmentalists are a mess. They demand, "How can you be so cruel?"

The hunter shrugs, "Hey, I can get quite a bit of money for that fox."

Lil asks, "How much money? How much money can you get for that fox? We'll pay you for the fox."

The hunter says, "Oh I can get thirty to fifty dollars for that pelt."

Negotiations begin, "Will you take forty dollars?"

The hunter agrees.

These career people then dive into their pockets and pull out money until they have enough to pay the hunter. I, of course, am not diving into my pockets for anything, because, first of all, there is nothing in my pockets, and second of all, I wasn't about to pay a hunter to take a fox out of his trap.

They hand him the money and he smiles even bigger. He's made a really good deal. The fox was going to get away, but it would still be in the valley. Chances are he'll catch that fox again and get himself another forty dollars.

I see the big grin on his face and grin back. He just stands there. The best is yet to come.

Now the fox belongs to the environmentalists, and they take a closer look at their newly acquired property. The animal is rabid with fear and pain. Not only is its hind leg stuck in this trap, but it's surrounded by the queerest smelling bunch of people it could ever hope to be afraid of. The fox snarled and bit at the poor environmentalists as they one-by-one reached timidly toward it, trying to figure out how to save it from the trap.

The hunter just stands there, watching. I stand there. Mitch shakes his head, amazed it is working out as well as it is.

The environmentalists try again, and one brave man inches toward the fox. Two women follow, cooing to the animal that they are friends come to help. Fox snarls and they jump back to their huddled group.

Finally, the hunter looks at me. I give him a shrug, "It's enough." In one smooth, experienced motion he takes off his coat, throws it over the fox, unhooks the latch, and opens the trap. Like a skilled matador he sweeps his coat from the wounded animal and fox shoots off at great speed.

It was over.

I thanked the hunter and shook his hand warmly. The environmentalists scurried together in their herd and marched back towards their log castle. Lil gave me a look of consternation. Whose side was I on, anyway? I had to laugh. Here were these environmentalists, so intent on saving the fox from the hunter, and yet it was only the hunter who knew the fox.

The hunter had lived with the fox. His hands had the feeling, his nose the smell. He knew how to live on the planet with it. The environmentalists wanted it as a pet.

It's this kind of attitude that makes it difficult to deal with our environmental problems. Everybody internalizes it too much. The fox was just a fox. The hunter was just a hunter.

The hunter needs to be treated with respect. The fox needs to be treated with respect as it is, not as we wish it to be.

If it is true that the only way we can have wilderness is to remove human beings from the scene of being natural—if that's true—then we have to close our wilderness off to all people. Otherwise, we have to manage the wilderness in a way that is also suitable for people. I wonder how many environmentalists would actually be for wilderness if even they were not allowed in it.

The other solution is to find the wild places within ourselves. Then there can be a blend of the wild of the world and the natural human being. To me, this is the only way we are going to have what we would call a sustainable ecology on our planet. We can't have the foxes and the spiders walking around being the representatives of all things natural. We have to be it ourselves.

Human beings are the most intelligent creatures on the planet at this time. This intelligence is an immense blessing for us and can be a blessing for everything else as well. To truly fulfill our ability—our creative and intelligent ability—we should work so that the places where human beings live are the most beautiful places on the planet. We are the most creative and the most intelligent, so we should also be the most beautiful. On the day that beauty and harmony become our coin of commerce, then we will have wilderness everywhere. Probably, I'll also have a job on that day.

Until then, don't waste time projecting your own insecurities onto the wild creatures. I remember driving home from the fox incident and arguing with Lil the whole time. She was so insistent that saving that one little fox—that individual fox, was such an important thing. I told her, no. There is no such thing as an individual fox as we think of individual people.

Even people are not individuals, as we think of individuals. Deep in the recesses of the mind, in that place where silence and truth dwells, is the realization that we are a blend of everything. We are not separate.

In reality there is no individual you. The idea seems scary, but it is where all blessings lie. The feeling of being separate, this feeling of "me," is the thing that makes us miserable. That is our disease. The fox does not have this disease, this hang-up, this separation between itself, its world, and all the other forces of the world.

If we were down to the very last fox and we took it and put it in a zoo, we would not have saved the fox. All we would have is a piece of DNA sitting in a cage. It wouldn't be fox any more. The fox and its environment are one. The fox doesn't need to be saved. Preserve the environment that sustains the fox, and fox will take care of himself, as he has always done.

It is obvious from the old stories that Native American Indians knew this. The stories never say that a particular fox came and said this and did that. The stories don't say "this fox," they say "fox." Fox himself came and spoke to the people. Coyote came and stole the bone, or raven picked up the stick and flew away. This is how the stories go. Quail taught me this on Beaver Creek.

In a very poignant way quail is not just quail. Quail is also food. Quail is food for something else that's being. And there are always enough quails because quails have just enough food and are enough food. That's what you call balance and harmony. This is why the wilderness is beautiful. Because everything is its own being, and yet, also food for something else.

We are no different from that. We are also food for something else. Mosquitoes live off of us. Think of all the things that live off of our waste. We are food for mice, for cockroaches. After we die, we are food for whatever can manage to eat embalming fluid. There is no way to get out of being what we are. We are one with the universe. We are food.

It's not so scary.

The purpose of the religious search is to get rid of this oppressive feeling of individuality. The goal in our hearts is to become one with God, because this feeling of separateness is a thorn in our side. That is the wound in our being.

I know this one thing totally. We don't have to save the planet because there is nothing wrong with the planet. All we have to do is save ourselves. If we are fine, everything else will be fine. The cure for separateness is gratefulness. Don't make your separateness bigger by projecting your feelings of separateness on the rest of the world. Get over it. Be grateful.

Chapter Twenty

What I Learned from Cougar

When I look back on my life with the animals I see three who have taught me major life lessons: mouse, deer, and cougar. I didn't go out in search of the lessons; I didn't even know that learning could happen in the way it did. These lessons were searching for me.

The natural world is there to teach those who have the knack of listening. Native peoples had this knack. It is not like going to the university to learn, because the teachers are tricky. It takes time. I've seen many people try to emulate Native American beliefs of learning from the animals, but they look for it too quickly. They want to go out and have a spirit quest and get a quick fix from the animals. You can't get it from a weekend workshop. My experience is that it takes a long time to learn a whole lesson from an animal. It takes a long relationship with the animal and you have to be awake.

It took twelve years for cougar to teach his lesson. First came the lesson from mouse and deer.

I learned from mouse because mouse always lived in my houses with me. In my little house on Beaver Creek mouse was king. He had lived there long before me, and is still there now that I am gone. He would come into my kitchen and do his best work to dirty my eating space. Everywhere mouse went he left his disease-filled black pellets. There was always the subtle smell of mouse. Where he left his pellets, I was certain he was also leaving mousy pee-pee and little hairs. There is no way you can eat food that has been visited by a mouse. Every time I found signs of mouse around my food I would have to throw it out to protect my family.

I did everything I could in my battle against mouse. I searched second-hand stores and garage sales for mouse-proof containers to hold rice, flour, and beans. I tried to keep my kitchen clean to prevent mouse from getting a good meal, filling his belly and happily reproducing in the hollows of my walls. All the same, many a time, I would go through a box of clothes, or a drawer, and find a mouse nest full of little pink babies. They looked like the plastic pigs that come in toy farm animal sets, only they wiggled.

I could never look as I killed nests of mouse babies. Without touching and feeling I wrapped them in paper and stuck the wad in a garbage bag, or tossed it quickly into the fire, trying not to think about what was happening.

During my years at Beaver Creek I got into reading New Age type books, which were concerned about advancing me spiritually. These New Age books convinced me that spiritual people are supposed to be totally pure: no negative thoughts, no fear, no jealousy, no bad personality stuff at all.

I couldn't live up to it. I tried to be good but I was still bad. Spiritual people were not supposed to kill anything—even mouse babies, or spiders that crawled up their legs. I was a vegetarian at the time and I wasn't supposed to kill *anything,* but I was confused because I had to kill mouse. If I didn't, mouse would appear everywhere, because my very act of living as a human being created mouse-breeding situations.

Little did I know, the mouse dilemma was only a symptom of a deeper malaise: the contradiction of what I thought of spirituality, and what I experienced of reality. I had set out on a spiritual path to purge myself of all nasty things. I thought that fear, anger, and jealousy were bad emotions. Purifying myself spiritually meant getting rid of these things. The reality of my practice was that I felt very negative about my negative thoughts; I started to be afraid of being afraid; I was jealous of people who appeared to not be jealous. Truthfully, I was a lot worse off than if I had only concerned myself with cleaning up mouse pellets.

I thought that animals were closer to nature, so therefore more pure than humans. Look at the birds; how freely they fly, seemingly without fear or care. The powerful wolf and wily coyote cruise through their world, totally aware of who they are. The deer is a picture of pure grace and balance. I revered these things as better, more natural than myself. I thought animals lived always happy and pure, in a state of grace.

Then, one evening, I was sitting on my couch and a mouse ran across the floor. It stopped and looked at me. Her eyes were huge and vibrating. I recognized fear in those big, round, black eyes. I moved. She darted for cover, her body shivering with fear.

I was amazed. Here was a totally natural animal. It was pure, and yet it was feeling fear—big time—and a good thing too, because I would have killed it in a heartbeat. Maybe I had been overly generous in my assessment of animal nature, for these little animals at least. That mouse was definitely afraid. It scurried, and it shook with fear. This moment stuck with me and I carried it for a few days.

I was outside; suddenly, there in front of me, was a doe. She stopped, and looked straight in my eyes. Her eyes were giant and luminous, vibrating. I saw the fear. The same fear as the mouse. This deer was bigger and more stately than the mouse, but her eyes were the same round blackness of fear. It was the same fear that was often in me. The only difference was that deer held her head high and aware with her fear, I tended to bow my head with fear.

Mouse had tried to teach me the lesson, but she was too small to be noticed. It took the deer, which I idolize, to bring the lesson home. Fear is a good thing. It is a time to watch carefully. Fear makes mouse scurry for cover; it keeps deer's ears alert for any noise, eyes attuned to movement. Fear and awareness are the same thing. The mouse must watch because I am going to try to kill it. The deer must also watch because if I don't try to kill it, something else will. I realized the dignity of fear and decided to allow myself my own fear, to even listen to it with head held high, eyes luminous. Maybe the many voices that spoke to me through my emotions were something to discover rather than something to avoid.

The lesson was bigger than that. If fear was an acceptable part of nature, then maybe jealousy, anger, and all that other stuff was also natural. I decided to allow myself all my pieces, whether they were labeled negative or not. From that moment I started honoring myself and keeping track of how my intricacies worked, instead of trying to shove the untidy pieces away. It is a more relaxing way to live, and more fun, although it makes me even more dangerous in polite company.

It's taken awhile, but I've grown into this way of living. Now I'm not jealous of people who don't appear to be jealous. I'm sorry for them. They miss an awareness twinge. I've discovered that all my pieces are a part of my personal ecology. Jealousy is a good thing if you learn how to use it well—sometimes you need it. Guilt is one of my favorites. It's the great motivator, urging me to do things that I would otherwise avoid. Fear keeps me alert. Anxiety makes me change. When I feel fear, I know I am facing something new, and I must need all my wits about me. When I honor all my pieces, I honor my self. This was the last secret of nature that turned me totally native. There is no going back.

Look closely at the birds. Even though they sing, they are not always joyous; the same is true of the coyote, and every other animal. They are just trying to get by, trying to make a living. They go through a lot of hassles in their day and deal with them as well as possible. Sometimes they play, and then the joy is there for all to share. This is the kind of joy I love; the joy that comes when the sun suddenly warms my back, or the water tastes wonderful. This kind of joy is never overcome by the so-called negative feelings that also flick in and out of attention.

That was the lesson of mouse and deer.

Cougar had another way of teaching. Cougar is almost invisible in the world because he is a night animal, and very quiet. Panther Creek and its, tributary Beaver Creek, where I lived, were good places for cougars, among the best in central Idaho.

I always knew there were cougars around. I had never seen one but had encountered their tracks on a number of occasions. The tracks are big. Whenever I found a set I would kneel and put my hand into the indentations, feeling the size. I couldn't imagine how big this animal must have been.

Down near us we had an old mountain-man type guy, named Leon, who made his living hunting, trapping, and gathering things from the wilderness: deer, elk and sheep horns, hides and snake skins. He made knife handles and hat bands. He would catch rattlesnakes by stepping on them with his boot, then slice off the head, throw the body over his shoulder, and keep walking down the trail. Sometimes I would go gathering with him. As with Ray Kelley I was interested in gathering information.

Leon showed me how the deer nested in the snow in the winter, how to follow cougar tracks, the time of the year and type of gully in which to find horns. Once we traveled up Beaver Creek and found a bloody spot in the snow where a deer had been killed. "This," he said, "is a cougar kill." He showed me how the cougar had dragged the kill to a hiding place. We looked around; no cougar to be found of course, but I felt cougar was watching us. I was always in full view of cougar, yet he remained silent to my life.

One day, I was getting my teeth worked on at the dentist's office in Salmon. It was a root canal, so there was plenty of time for Dr. Smith to talk, and of course, I couldn't say a thing, my mouth being full of teeth grindings and rubber bands. Dr. Smith was an avid hunter and friend with the folks at the Fish and Game. A mother cougar had been shot down on Panther Creek, just a few miles from my home—some stupid hunter had shot a mama with cubs. All through my grinding, mouth open wide, I received a blow-by-blow account of his trip with the Fish and Game guys to catch the cubs—trying to save them from certain death in the wilderness. Three cubs had been rescued. They were in a cage down at the Fish and Game offices.

With Dr. Smith talking and me grunting yeses, he assured me, and convinced me that I should go by the Fish and Game and take a look at the cubs. After all, they used to live one draw over from my house. We were neighbors, the cubs and I; the Fish and Game wouldn't mind. "Tell them I sent you."

With my face swollen from the Novocain, and dragging my own kids by my side, I stopped by the Fish and Game offices on my way back out of town, heading home to Panther Creek. I was led to a stout cage built onto a trailer. I walked up and looked in, half expecting to see some cute little kittens. Hissing teeth and raw muscle lunged at the bars of the cage. Three huge animals hated me, then slunk back into the cage up against the back wall in defiance. Sharp teeth, millions of sharp teeth. Claws backed with sinewy muscle. Tight, hard. There was no question of making friends with these fellows. These were no kitty cats.

My body reacted of its own accord; blood stopped; hairs stood up on bare arms. My eyes were round, vibrating. Head up. This was the wildest thing I'd ever seen, these cougar cubs were pure teeth, muscle, and kill. Trapped in a cage, showing their rage.

I realized that this was a reality that lived right next to my house! The invisible had become the known. Looking into the cage I felt a new kind of fear that was borne out of total respect. This kind of wildness was not a thing the mind could argue with. My mind was stopped by the respect of pure awe.

I didn't stay long. There was too much dignity in those cubs to stare at them like circus attractions. I left my neighbors with a deep silence. They would be raised and returned to the wilderness. I also returned to the wilderness with a new understanding of the awesome forces that swirled in harmony around me.

I now walked two miles down my road to get the mail with a new feeling of awareness—fear. Not that I thought cougars were going to attack me any moment; the odds were against that. But I now *knew* cougar. My eyes were rounder, blacker. I was more awake. When I encountered cougar tracks I felt their size with my hand, fully understanding the breadth of those clawed feet.

One day my friend, Annie, came to visit. My house was two miles up Beaver Creek from the Panther Creek Road. Our road was pretty narrow, steep and tough. So Annie parked her car down at Panther Creek and walked up. We didn't get to see each other too often, living miles apart, and having no phones, so we had a wonderful visit, weeding out in my garden, eating dinner, talking until it got dark.

I asked Annie to spend the night, but she thought her husband might worry, so she finally decided it was time to go home. Problem was, she was afraid to walk two miles in the dark alone. There was barely a moon, but there were lots of stars. It wasn't very light, but was not totally dark either. I thought a walk in the night would be a fun adventure and convinced Annie I could walk her to her car. I grabbed a flashlight, one of those headband types, and we took off walking. We talked and enjoyed the stars and the two miles passed quickly, our little flashlight making a comfortable lighted spot on the road in front of our steps.

Annie got in her car, waved, and drove off. I turned around to walk back.

Suddenly it seemed much darker and quieter than before. My blood remembered what it felt like to be frozen when I looked at the cougars. I felt respect. I could feel my eyes bulging forward in the darkness. My ears twitched, listening for the slightest sound.

The flashlight interfered with my vision by capturing my sight to the disk of light in front of me. I could see nothing in the distance. I felt vulnerable and illuminated. I turned off the flashlight and let my night vision lead me through the darkness, feet hurrying on the familiar road.

I couldn't see cougar; I never could. Cougar could see me if cougar wanted.

I wasn't really afraid, as in being terrified. After all, I had walked this road for years. But I was aware and full of respect. I felt every breath that went in and out of my lungs, and felt every rise and dip in the road as my feet touched with their footprints. I made my way home. The feeling was one of being very alive and part of the air. I felt juicy and delicious, like I would make a good meal. It wasn't a horrible feeling, but rather more like a sense of belonging. I was part of the great web of life. Cougar could eat me if cougar wanted.

Years passed and I moved into Salmon so the kids could go to school. After breaking up with John, I had other relationships that didn't work. I experienced heartbreak, abandonment, neglect, and deception from lovers and friends, all those things that have become typical for modern man. Sometimes I felt entirely lost in trying to understand why people treat others the way they do. Where are the human beings? The true people?

Town is much harder than wilderness for living. I felt disconnected, unwelcome. Talking is so often unkind; expectations are too high. I felt like an invisible person, unable to be heard by the people who mattered to me. The breakup of my last relationship left me isolated, with a broken heart. I couldn't understand how I could be treated like I didn't exist. Only the insignificant parts of me were accepted in the human world. It was very undignified. I continued to work and take care of the things that needed to be done. I continued to watch; once your eyes become round with awareness, they don't easily fall into forgetfulness even if being awake means feeling pain.

At this time I was making money by typing resumes for people. Rodney came to get his resume done. He was an Indian, full blood, one of the last of the Lemhi, the tribe that had lived in the Salmon valley. He was thin and taut. Rodney was wild, and his eyes flashed as he talked; they were big and round and black, and I could look into the depths of them. His old grandfather had raised him in the traditional Indian ways, which emphasized family values and honor. His wildness struggled with the modern world: the difficulty of making a living, the insensitive ways of relating.

He had fallen in and out of alcoholism. He told me about breaking up with his girlfriend. She had flirted with other men, an act that dishonored and hurt him. She was in bed with another guy the *day* he left; unthinkable.

I talked gingerly with Rodney, careful of how I spoke, feeling his wildness, aware of the fact that he was volatile, that he deserved to be treated with respect. We worked with difficulty on his resume, trying to express his qualities to a world that didn't understand him. He had things he wanted to say to people. He needed to learn to express himself. I invited him to our writer's group the next Thursday. He came.

At the writer's group, first hand, I saw Rodney's inability to fit into the modern world. He was struggling to talk; it was mildly embarrassing. His anger had nowhere to go except into frustration. He came to the group twice. The second time, after he left, we talked about him. Florence wanted to know if she dared to ask him about Indian artifacts that she was trying to paint. I was sure that asking would give Rodney offense. In an off-hand manner, not even thinking what I meant, I said, "I'd watch out. He's dangerous."

Flushed silence filled the room. The women, straightening the chairs, looked at me with big eyes. "What do you mean, 'He's dangerous?'" They had felt it too.

I didn't know right away.

It took me two days of wondering and remembering. Then my memory matched Rodney's taunt, pacing body with the cougars. My muscles responded to the image.

I felt the same thing in myself. I was wild. Everyone is. That's why fits of rage can pour out of me. That's why my stomach restricts when people don't see my magnificence and treat me as if I "should" be something else. I'm a beast that was formed in the wild jungles of Africa. I want to run away when something scares me. I want to run towards things that attract me. I am an immense harmony of urges and awareness. I conceive pain and pleasure and at the same time, and give birth to them. All the pieces of my being fit into a divine puzzle that can emit love or spit the fire of hate. I like what I am.

I saw these same qualities in all people. I realized it was a matter of respect. Fear is awareness and fear is also respect. It wasn't just Rodney who was wild and dangerous. It was all of us. In Rodney and cougar, and perhaps in me, the wildness is on the surface. It's easy to see. Many people grovel with their pain. Wildness wears pain with head high, eyes aware. We all have that kind of fierceness within. It's there, close to the surface, even though it has been homogenized by modern life.

This is the secret of relationships with others. This is why our modern relationships are pale and uncommitted. We see each other as tame pets; and we aren't. We are deep pools of the unexpected.

We think we know our spouses or our friends because we have become familiar with them—we lose the fear of the unknown and we lose respect. But we should watch out! Wild parts can leap out at unexpected moments. Then we think something has gone wrong. But maybe, really, something has just gone right. Maybe we should be just a little bit more afraid of each other, and a lot more aware.

We should treat each other as if we were all dangerous. Cougar showed me this kind of morality: the art of treating each other with awe.

Chapter Twenty-One

Walking without Footprints

So now I can barely talk to anyone because I've lost the idea that there is something wrong with the world. Out in nature things die, they eat each other, they scream when they are hurt and they never clean up after themselves—and yet everything is okay. Water is beautiful and pure evil at the same time. It can be soft and warm, it can crack you with its cold, or it can destroy with sudden sheer force—but really, it is only water. Even invisible things, like air and gravity, can grab you when you least expect it and take away your next choice—but what was that choice going to be anyway?

Living too long in the landscape is dangerous. It's big and wild there, and a person can become that world to the point where all the chaos inside is no more a problem than the chaos outside. Thoughts are a wind that sometimes blows hot, and sometimes blows cold from the north. Emotions are water trickling softly and glinting in the sunlight, until it hits the white raging rapids.

We aren't such a big mystery, you and I. And knowing that can really get a girl into trouble. How can I possibly remember, during every conversation, that people are guarded and possessive of things inside themselves that they don't like? How can I remember what not to say?

My life, now, is seen with the eyes of deer and mouse. I'm always watching. I watch myself and find that this makes authentic living mandatory. With just this simple watching I learn that emotions are nothing more than sensation, and thoughts no more important than the summer breeze. My being is the universe through which these breezes blow.

The pure way to live is with wide eyes—whether of amazement or fear, it doesn't matter. I am such a small thing in space and time when considered by myself. The mountains can hardly even blink to know I have passed, and the stars haven't a clue. My footprints are swept away as quickly as I make them.

The many things that stir inside me are things I really need to *be* me. All philosophies about peace and love have fled as I live in a river of time that simply possesses the moment.

The problem with me now, is that I've gone completely native. I walked into the wilderness, all those many years ago, to find a way to be an authentic human, and it wasn't all that hard to find. I was lucky in my guess that the answer to these crazy questions lay inside me, somewhere, hidden under the many layers that modern society had put upon me.

And now, as I see it, there is much to do.

Mankind is poised in a moment of decision, where we have to come up with new ways of living. There is not a firm answer from the past to save us, and every step forward is going to create another unknown. We can't get stuck on silly details like how to wash our clothes, or which recipe is best, or whether or not mountain men should wear pants every day. There is a seed inside every heart that knows how to watch with luminous eyes and how to howl at the moon.

This is the greatest time to be alive.

Afterward

Did you enjoy this journey? A photo album can be viewed at http://www.mysticdance.com.

0-595-24660-5